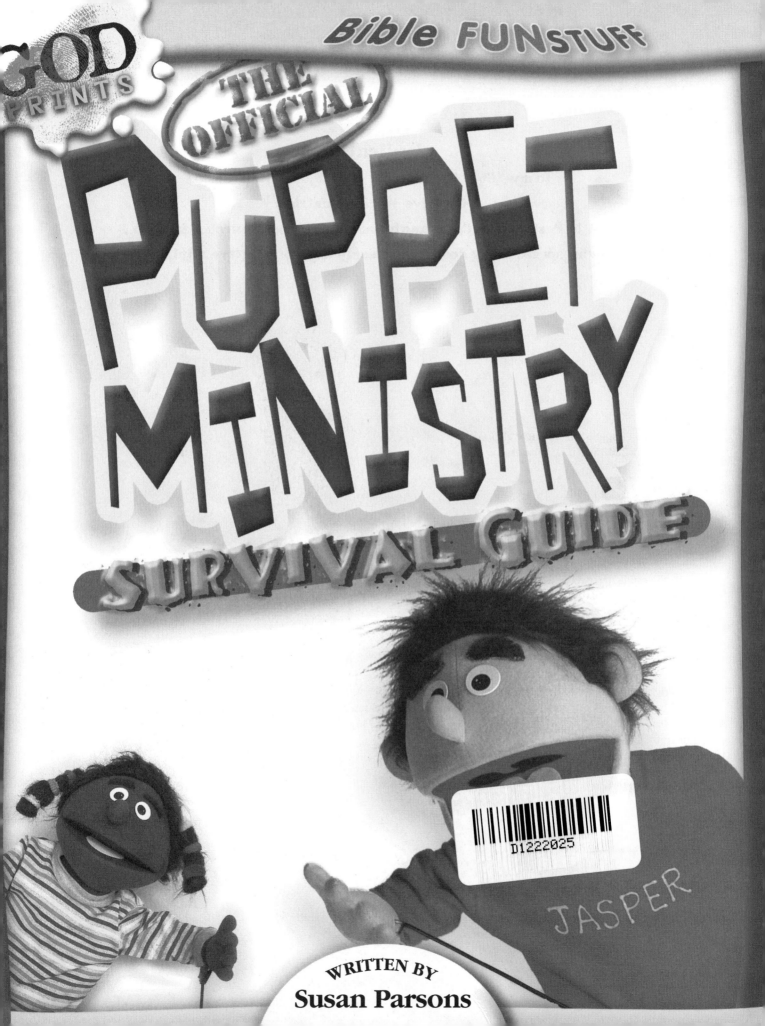

Dedication

To my "Good Samaritan," Rev. Sylvia R. Evans of
Creative Word Ministries;
and to Pastor Mike Cavanaugh and Elim Gospel Church, Lima, NY,
who opened many doors in my early days of creative ministry.

The Official Puppet Ministry Survival Guide
Copyright © 2002 Susan D. Parsons

Published by Cook Communications Ministries

Edited by: Lois Keffer
Art Direction: Mike Riester
Cover Design: Peter Schmidt, Granite Design
Interior Design: Dana Sherrer, iDesignEtc.
Illustrations: Aline Heiser

Printed in the United States

First printing, 2002
1 2 3 4 5 6 7 8 9 10   06 05 04 03 02 01

ISBN 0781438411

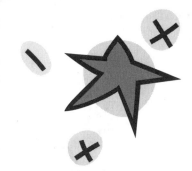

TABLE OF CONTENTS

Introduction 4

1 The Power of Puppets 5

2 You Made a Puppet from *What?* 13

3 Where Do You Think You're Going With THAT Script? 21

4 Recruiting Puppet People 33

5 Tricks of the Trade 41

6 Dress Up and Set the Stage 49

7 Building a PVC Pipe Stage 59

8 Make A Scene! 67

9 Sound, Lights and Special Effects 77

10 Puppet Patterns 85

11 Puppet Skit: Jasper's Disaster 101

12 Puppet Skit: It's Not Neat To Cheat 107

Introduction

I can do everything through him who gives me strength (Philippians 4:13)

Puppets are little clowns, meant to entertain rather than teach, right? WRONG! Puppets give you an open door to speak to kids of all ages—a door that is usual barred to "real people." Why? Because puppets are imaginative little make-believe people and critters with funny voices and faces. They don't deliver intellectual, three-point sermons. They're not harsh or threatening or preachy.

The world of puppet ministry can seem like a maze of confusing options. Take heart! This book will point you in the right direction. You're holding enough information to help you survive and thrive with puppets, and create a healthy and effective Christian ministry that serves your church and your community.

You don't have to be a professional actor to minister through puppets. You don't have to be good at being in front of people at all (thanks to the curtain!). You just have to be able to hold up your arm and wiggle your fingers. You'd be amazed at the personalities you can slip on when you don't have to show your face!

I've based every page of this book on personal experience and conviction. As a traveling creative ministry director licensed through Elim Fellowship of Lima, N.Y., I discovered many of these survival techniques the hard way—by making mistakes and having to fix them myself!

Later, I learned the finer points of scriptwriting while earning my M.A. in Communication at Regent University. Some lessons were tough: I used too many characters in my plays, I had to think "outside the box," and I needed to stop assuming that the whole world understood the language of the church. That was quite an awakening for a "veteran" Christian playwright and puppeteer, but it was necessary to move my work with puppets from mediocre to memorable. And now I can pass these lessons on to you!

This book can help you build your ministry from the ground up, or serve as a compass to refine your focus and technique. Here's your guide to finding a world of fulfilling ministry with little "creatures of the cloth"!

Discover the power of puppets in ministry. You'll be amazed to find how God uses your hands and your voice to touch and transform souls with his power!

chapter ONE

The Power of Puppets

So is my word that goes out from my mouth: It will not return to me empty, but will accomplish what I desire and achieve the purpose for which I sent it (Isaiah 55:11).

PUPPETS ARE CHARMING AND DISARMING—frosting on the children's-ministry cake. But because their message works its way right into hearts and minds, puppets are in a unique position to speak truth to kids and adults alike. Here's my own real-life example.

PUPPETS IN PRISON

It was a miracle! I'd been invited to bring my puppets and all their gear to one of Georgia's most tightly locked juvenile detention homes. My fellow puppeteer and I peeked through tiny holes where the curtains came together and saw about 20 of the hardest-looking teens you could imagine.

I remember one in particular, because I wondered what such a little guy could have done to require being so heavily guarded. He was flanked by two heavily muscled officers. The slight-framed boy stood against the back wall with heavy chains on his hands and feet. Then I learned the boy was there for shooting a man two days before. The wounded man was teetering on the edge of life and death, as was the future of the teenager who had pulled the trigger. And here I was about to do a puppet show!

The contrast in our situations almost made me feel silly. So, taking a deep breath, I consciously trusted in God to have a plan. I took comfort in being well prepared, both spiritually and professionally.

Most of the boys leaned back in their metal chairs with their arms folded, smirking as they waited for the mandatory show to begin. These tough street guys were visibly insulted by our childish-looking display—a six by six-foot puppet stage with bright blue curtains and a plywood sceneboard that looked like a little girl's dreamhouse. It was a kitchen, built to scale, with a little refrigerator that opened. There was even flowered wallpaper on the wall. The boys snickered in comic, adolescent, croaks, somewhere between soprano and buzz-saw. But I had done this enough to not be offended by their expressions of disdain. I knew what was about to happen.

I launched into the show. Jasper, my main puppet character, was a little boy about to get into trouble. With rod arms, he moved realistically to his pre-recorded voice and interacted with the other characters. When Jasper started listening to the puppet who enticed him to ignore the

His eyes burned an imprint into my soul: God can use the "foolishness" of puppetry to communicate the good news of Jesus Christ to ANYONE!

rules, the "captive" audience chuckled—they could relate.

Mid-show I peeked through the curtain. I could see a few boys beginning to lean forward with interest. Jasper was about to disobey his mom and use the blender to make a milkshake. When he did, he forgot to put on the lid and, with a special effect you'll read about later, the milkshake went everywhere—on his face, in his hair, all over his clothes and on the wall! And EVERY boy sitting in the room was leaning forward on the edge of his seat! The room full of teenagers in trouble with the law identified with Jasper's bad choice and the disastrous consequences. Jasper was splattered with the evidence of his bad choice. And matters got worse when his mom came home early. Jasper was busted!

This unlikely little puppet with a mission got through to some of the toughest boys in the Atlanta area. Suddenly they were open to the Word of God. They were eager to hear to hear how Jasper would get out of it. But Jasper didn't get out of it! Instead he repented, and the message hit homes.

At the close of the show the boys had their heads bowed. I asked for those who wanted to get right with God to simply open their eyes and look at me. More than half of them did. The boy standing in chains was among them. His eyes burned an imprint into my soul: God can use the "foolishness" of puppetry to communicate the good news of Jesus Christ to ANYONE!

SO WHAT'S THE SECRET?

Part of the secret is a little thing with a big name: anthropomorphism—the attribution of human characteristics to an animal or thing. A cloth-and–foam puppet boy like Jasper is already a human representation, but he's anthropomorphic in that he's still a *thing* to which human qualities are given. Anthropomorphism is the reason for the appeal of hundreds of cartoon characters, from Tweetie Bird® to Veggie Tales®. If you think about it, even Mickey Mouse‰ would be a dull little rodent without his

Our defenses come down. We're transported to an imaginary world of colorful, wacky creatures who aren't likely to lecture us; aren't likely to let us down.

human stance, speech and mannerisms, and his human boy wardrobe.

Most of us have used anthropomorphism to some degree. Say you're with a fussy baby who just won't settle down. What do you do? Grab the nearest inanimate object and, without a moment's thought, bring it to life. By so doing, you become a puppeteer. It might be a spoon that you transform into a hopping, peeping spoon-person. Or you might just use your fingers as wiggling, talking people. The fascinated baby calms down to watch the show. Voila! The power of puppetry!

Children love anthropomorphic characters for several reasons. First of all, children subconsciously view animals as safe creatures under their dominion. From the time a child is born, we put animal toys and dolls in the bassinet. We point out horsies and birdies through the car window. Nearly all children are attracted to soft, licking puppies and gentle, purring kittens. Cats and puppies, frogs, little furry mice—even big-eared, clumsy elephants are their friends.

Jesus is the one with power to transform hearts and lives. As a puppeteer, you have a marvelous opportunity to be the voice through which he may choose to speak.

When these creatures don human qualities, such as speech and clothing, their friendship potential multiplies. Children listen to them. Even grown-ups listen to them! Our defenses come down. We're transported to an imaginary world of colorful, wacky creatures who aren't likely to lecture us; aren't likely to let us down. We watch and listen with open hearts as they impart truth in fun little parables. Although we have to leave that imaginary world when the show is over, the truths remain.

Is there a problem with creating animal and puppet characters who think and talk and react like people? Well, there was *one* talking animal in the Bible— Balaam's donkey! A puppet is simply a different kind of mouthpiece. Puppet skits are slices of life—parables that put important truths about Jesus in a form that even little children can receive.

Think for a minute about the significant symbolic role animals play in the Bible. Jesus is the Lion of Judah, the Lamb of God. God's people are the sheep of his pasture. Unbelievers are goats. Ants are examples of hard work. Birds of the air have "no worries." The list goes on and on. Jesus himself used animals as a metaphor to convey spiritual truths. And he used parables—simple stories with many levels of meaning—to teach his disciples. Let's follow his example!

JESUS, THE POWER SOURCE

Jesus is the one with power to transform hearts and lives. As a puppeteer, you have a marvelous opportunity to be the voice through which he may choose to speak. You're a walking, talking visual aid—the voice and movement of a humorous or poignant character with a special delivery of truth.

Your role as a puppeteer will vary from script to script. You may be a preacher, teacher, example, exhorter, encourager, comforter or prophet. You're like an Aaron, speaking the words of Moses. You're a messenger. When you speak God's truth, you become a conduit for his power.

THE MONEY SOURCE?

Budget constraints put a big road block in the way of many children's ministry dreams. Not so with puppets. If your ministry can afford elaborate puppets and sets, count your blessings! But take heart if you're working on a minimal budget: you can do amazing things in puppetry with very little investment at all. Honest! You can use your fingers and a washable marker; an old sock with wiggly eyes peering over a sheet strung between two chairs; even a toilet plunger (a brand new one!) with mop hair and eyes made of ping-pong balls or painted walnuts attached with hot glue. Whatever you have around you will do. The key is to do it with gusto. Your enthusiasm, love for kids and dedication to Christ will shine through!

> "Whatever your hand finds to do, do it with all your might."
> Ecclesiastes 9:10

INVEST YOURSELF

You can make a big impact with a tiny budget, but being a puppet ministry leader does require an investment of energy and creativity. Do the job requirements below suit you?

- A strong desire to share spiritual truth
- A great love for kids
- Creativity and resourcefulness—being able to make something out of nothing
- A willingness to invest time in preparation
- An ability to think like a child and have fun!

If you have these qualities, you're ready to roll!

REMEMBER THIS!

If I could pass on only one thing I've learned to those ministering to children it would be this: Children aren't just pesky little irritants who will forget you someday. Children are little people with keen minds.

We presented the Gospel through drama and puppetry, and thousands of kids trusted in Jesus.

In 10 years or less, some of them will be defending you in our armed forces. Some may be drawing your blood in the doctor's office. Others could be teaching your grandchildren. And they'll remember the adults who took time to guide them in their spiritual journey.

More than 15 years ago, I toured parts of New York and the Eastern U.S. with my teenage troupe of actors and puppeteers. We presented the Gospel through drama and puppetry, and thousands of kids trusted in Jesus. As I witnessed their prayers of faith, I wondered if these were truly life changing moments, or if the kids who responded were just intrigued by the puppet sets and costumed characters.

Ten years later I began getting letters and reports from college students who told me that they trusted their lives to Christ at one of my puppet presentations a decade before! Those wiggly, giggly little people under constructions were now adults building families of their own. What a feeling of satisfaction to that God had used my puppets and plays to change their lives! At the very outset of your puppet ministry, ask God to help you see with eyes of faith the good results that are to come.

"Let us not become weary in doing good, for at the proper time we will reap a harvest if we do not give up."
Galatians 6:9

ROAD WARRIORS

Have puppets, will travel! With a little creative thinking, you can discover wonderful ministry venues for your little "creatures of the cloth."

Children are an obvious audience for puppet ministries. In your church, puppet programs are perfect for Children's Church, Vacation Bible School, Sunday School, harvest parties, Christmas programs and church picnics.

Children are an obvious audience for puppet ministries. In your church, puppet programs are perfect for Children's Church, Vacation Bible School, Sunday School, harvest parties, Christmas programs and church picnics.

You might consider ministering outside your church as a pro bono outreach to other children. Develop a few programs for a general, non-church public to get you in the door and establish community relationships. You may be able to secure a network of interested parties who would like you to bring your complete package to their organization. Meanwhile, your expression of love and care through your puppet programs can bring a lot of needed joy to kids in:

☺ Children's Hospitals—especially during holidays, puppeteers and other entertainers are very welcome. Depending on the rules of the hospital, you may have to "tone down" your Christian message, but don't fight it. God can do wonders as you just give a cup of cold water in his name.

☺ Foster care—call your local Department of Social Services and ask to speak to a foster care supervisor. They frequently hold picnics and other events for foster children, and usually seek puppeteers. Again, the public nature of the organization may require you to refrain from performing a blatantly Christian message, but you'll get your foot in the door.

☺ Day care—many day care centers would love to have puppeteers come in. Make sure your material is suitable for the very, very young.

With the right scripts, you can be a welcome addition to the agenda at men's retreats, women's meetings, mother-daughter banquets, and other specialized events. Almost any dramatic skit can be adapted to puppets, and pre-recorded for convenience and the assurance of being heard.

Seniors make up some of the best audiences in terms of attention and feedback. Nursing homes, retirement homes, or just senior church groups may enjoy watching some tailor-made puppet programs humorously and tastefully depicting the wisdom and vast experience of the aged.

Don't forget singles ministries. Puppets can provide great comic relief for icebreakers. And most singles-themed skits can be acted out by puppets as well as human beings. Sometimes they can be more fun to watch, too!

When fairs and festivals are held in your area, call your Chamber of Commerce or other hosting organization to find out whether you can rent a booth to set up a puppet show. You should be free to perform whatever program you wish at these outdoor events, but always check to make sure.

Seek permission to hold shows at:
- Libraries
- Parking Lots
- Bookstores
- Schools
- Fundraisers

Be prepared to do non-religious programs at public facilities, and do so without complaint. Some of your audiences might be curious about other aspects of your ministry, and new doors may open. Meanwhile, there's nothing wrong with teaching basic good citizenship or entertaining by acting out a storybook as a community service. It could be the start of something that God uses in wonderful ways!

chapter two You Made a Puppet from What?

Whatever you do, whether in word or deed, do it all in the name of the Lord Jesus, giving thanks to God the Father through him.
(Colossians 3:17)

ALL PUPPETS ARE NOT CREATED EQUAL! Some are made of socks, some of paper bags, some of plush fabric, some of wood, and some of high-quality, molded, synthetic materials with elaborate, hand-painted faces. Puppets range in price from 10 cents (the garage-sale sock) to hundreds of dollars. While your church ministry may not be able to afford the hundreds-of-dollars variety, take heart. You can make wonderful puppets with scrap materials and a little time and imagination. You'll find lots of ideas and patterns for puppet making throughout this book.

To get you started in your quest for the perfect puppet, let's do a quick overview of the variety of puppets and how you can get your hands on (and in!) them.

HAND PUPPETS

Hand puppets are the most common type. You'll see lots of adorable ones in toy departments and card shops. The two sub-types of hand puppets are easy to remember. Just think of the kinds of hand gear they resemble:

Mitten puppets
Glove puppets

Both types have an effective place in the puppet world; however, the moving mouth puppet offers a greater degree of human-like attributes, so young audiences usually prefer them.

The late Shari Lewis' glorified-sock puppet, Lambchop®, has a moveable mouth but no moveable arms, and is as charming a puppet as has ever "lived"! The window to Lambchop's "feelings" was her mouth, which Lewis masterfully contorted into all kinds of expressions, from smiles and frowns to an adorable lip bite when Lambchop® was uncertain.

Glove puppets (moving arms/no mouth) can be very cute and effective as "sidekicks" or secondary, supportive characters, but should probably be mute characters when they're used in conjunction with talking puppets whose mouths move. Sticking to mute characters for puppets with non-moving mouths helps keep audiences from being distracted.

ROD-ARM PUPPETS

Rod-arm puppets are my personal favorite because they offer a moving mouth and moving arms at the same time. Removable thin rods approximately 18 inches long attach to the wrists of the puppets. While the puppeteer works the mouth with one hand, the other hand manipulates the puppet's hands with rods—together or one at a time, depending on the level of skill.

Rod-arm puppets may be purchased from a variety of puppet makers for prices ranging in average from $50 to $150. They're also easier to make than you would imagine! If you just can't wait to see how, peek ahead to Chapter 10.

ROD ARM PUPPETS WITH LEGS

Why not go for the whole banana? If you add legs to your rod-arm puppets, you can carry them around with the legs draped over your arm. Sound complicated? It's not!

Use a seam ripper to open the seam of the pants in the back, just above the crotch. Open about 5 inches of the seam.

Now, whenever you want to use your puppet without a stage, you can carry him or seat him on a table next to you. Just slip the elastic pants around the puppet's "waist", pin them for safety, and slip your arm into the hole under the puppet. (It's easier than dressing a fussy baby!)

HUMAN HAND PUPPETS

Human hand puppets require two persons to operate. They are larger than ordinary puppets, with sleeves and gloves for human arms and hands. One person works the mouth and one of the arms/hands, while another person works the leftover appendage.

You'll need:

- ↻ A pair of elastic-waist baby slacks in size 12 months
- ↻ A pair of canvas baby sneakers, about size 2
- ↻ A pair of infant's tights (1-6 months)
- ↻ Polyester fiberfill
- ↻ Needle and thread

Lightly stuff baby tights with fiberfill. Stuff the feet into the sneakers and hand-stitch them in place. Also, stitch the waist together from side to side. Slip the pants over the tights and shoes. Sew the waist of the tights to the inside front waistband of the slacks.

It requires a considerable amount of teamwork to synchronize the gestures of a human hand puppet. But the effort is worth the payoff—these puppets can be very lifelike. They make great storytellers or key characters, such as an old wise man or a storekeeper.

One of the coolest things about this genre of puppet is that they can grasp. Human hand puppets can pick up things, write, pour, stack—almost anything you normally do with your hands. You can make a human hand puppet by adding a shirt and gloves to a large-headed puppet.

FINGER PUPPETS

Finger puppets are ineffective when the audience is so large that the puppets are too far away to be seen. But for smaller, intimate groups, they can be terrific additions to your program!

Finger puppets are best used in groups of their own kind, or as tiny supportive characters (such as a worm or bug). In such cases, kids tend to overlook their lack of a mouth!

You may purchase finger puppets (some real cuties can be found in gift shops), or create

your own by "dressing up" your fingers with faces, hair, hats, dresses, etc. Short programs with well-dressed finger puppets can be a wonderfully effective break in long puppet programs, if used skillfully.

You've probably drawn puppet faces on your fingers when you were a kid, bored out of your mind in math class. A length of

finger from a knit glove makes a wonderful sweater. Use the finger tip of the glove for a matching hat! Kids are mesmerized when you draw and dress your finger puppets right on the spot. Use a spur-of-the-moment pair of finger puppets to settle a rowdy class. They're always at your fingertips!

MARIONETTES

The art of puppeteering with marionettes (stringed puppets, like Pinocchio) is a skilled specialty that is almost extinct in the United States. But if you have a particular interest in them, and care to spend the time

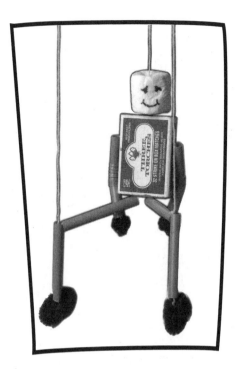

in practice, string puppets can add wonderful effects to your program some. What could be more fun than seeing your puppets run, fly and jump?

While most marionettes are quite complex, this book includes instructions for a simple marionette you can make from straws! See the page 89.

MECHANICAL MOUTH PUPPETS

You can turn almost any stationary object into a puppet by giving it a moveable mouth. Really! There are several simple ways to create a moveable mouth. You'll find them explained in detail in Chapter 10. One of my favorites is the rubber band mouth.

You simply glue half of a rubber band in a straight line to any flat surface. Tie a thread to the center of the loose half of the rubber band. When you pull the thread down, the mouth opens. When you release the thread, the mouth "closes".

"WHATEVER" PUPPETS

If you study anything long enough, you can begin to see ways to make it a "living, breathing" puppet. Take the spoon puppet we mentioned in the introduction. Bop it around with a bit of whimsy and infants are fascinated!

The Godprints editorial team at Cook Communications Ministries has toyed with a variety of puppet possibilities over the years while developing our curriculum line. Most recently, writer/editor Mary Grace Becker came up with the simple idea of sticking a potato on a stick and adding facial features with brads, buttons, or anything else we could find. They're adorable, and are used in the Godprints Summer 2003 preschool curriculum.

Marketing Director Kerry Park dubbed them, "Puppets with A-*peel*"!

Godprints Director, Lois Keffer, has a brilliant, creative mind and is known for being unconventional. I didn't know just how well she thinks outside of the box until we took a trip together to a hardware store. Every aisle, to her, was full of potential puppets! "Look at that car scrubber," she said with the excited face of a three-year-old at the zoo. "It's just begging for a face!" I had to blink a couple of times, but eventually I could imagine a whimsical ministry tool being created from the blue-haired little scrub brush on a stick. That same season, we collaborated on a variation on the scrub brush theme and used it in the Godprints curriculum for Summer, 2002!

The message here is this: You can look anywhere and find a puppet. If your ministry is short of funds, be creative and invent your own fun characters! You'll find all the help you need in Chapter 10.

FUNDRAISING FOR PUPPETS

If your knees shake at the thought of raising funds for your puppet ministry, worry not! There are several non-aggressive techniques that are very effective for getting the resources you need.

People tend to like to donate money to specific, tangible needs rather than a blanket need for ministry funds. When I needed puppets and the donations just weren't coming in, I created a flyers to insert in the church bulletin and to send to our ministry constituents. Within 30 days, I had more than a dozen sponsors! The flyer I used included a picture of a sample puppet and said something like this:

The message here is this: You can look anywhere and find a puppet!

If you already have some puppets (or could borrow some) or if you need more puppets and equipment, ask the pastor to allow you to do a fundraising skit during the church service or between services in the foyer. You'll have more success if you refrain from doing a "fundraising skit" *per se*. They're not usually very entertaining. Instead, show the audience that you're able to communicate spiritual truth with puppets. When the skit is over, let the pastor tell the congregation how they can sponsor a puppet. You might take a special collection, set out a couple of puppet "hats" have special envelopes on the pew racks.

SPONSOR a PUPPET!

For a donation of only $ ___ you can sponsor a professional puppet who will be used regularly in communicating the Word of God to young and old! You will receive a photo and brief biography of the puppet character you sponsor. Puppets will be the property of ___ and will travel near and far to spread the Good News! Just fill out the form below and make your checks payable to ___

SPONSOR A PUPPET Contribution Form

Name _____

Address _____

City _____ State _____ Zip _____

Phone _____ Email _____

I will sponsor ___ puppet(s) at $ _____ each.

Total enclosed: $ _____

You can always hold the traditional car washes, bake sales, rummage sales and bazaars to raise funds. Even if your raise enough money for one puppet, it will be the effort. The more puppets you can obtain and employ with excellence and creativity, the more people will want to support the ministry.

chapter three Where Do You Think You're Going With That Script?

The unfolding of your words gives light;
it gives understanding to the simple.
(Psalm 119:130)

NOW THAT YOU HAVE FUNNY LITTLE FELLOWS...who look so believable when their mouths move with your hands, what are they going to say? Something that will make a positive spiritual impact! The time we have for children's ministry is significantly less than the time kids have to watch TV. A little 5- to 15-minute skit may be your window of opportunity to share spiritual truth with kids who might not get it any other way. The Bible says,

> "Conduct yourselves with wisdom toward outsiders making the most of the opportunity"
>
> (Colossians 4:4).

Use wisdom in selecting your puppet scripts, to make the most out of the opportunity! Make sure your scripts are redemptive, and not just entertaining dialogue designed to keep kids sitting still. Here are the key things you need to know to create scripts that pack a scriptural punch.

BRING THE TRUTH TO LIFE!

The truth of the Gospel needs to be thoughtfully and carefully conveyed. A silly script may keep your kids entertained, but it won't get the truth where you want it to go. Fun sets and special effects will open the door, but a strong script is what carries the truth home.

STICK TO YOUR PLAN

As much as we love off-the-cuff humor and quick quips, pre-written scripts with well-timed humor can ensure that your message will be clear and fun to follow. Take the time to select good scripts or write your own. Then you and your puppeteers will be confident of where the script is going and what part each person plays. And you won't have any giggling behind the stage or frantic whispers of, "Say something! I don't know what to do!"

You'll find some great puppet scripts to get you going, starting on p. 101 of this book. Recording scripts on tape will totally eliminate the risk of dropping lines—unless your tape player breaks down!

Many good puppet scripts are also available in Christian bookstores or online by a variety of ministries and publishers. There are also lots of good puppet script books at your local Christian book store. Here are two of my online recommendations:

- ℮ One-Way Street
  (www.onewaystreet.com)
- ℮ Puppet Productions, Inc.
  (www.puppetproductions.com)
- ℮ UpWrite Productions
  (www.puppetrax.com)

3 STEPS TO GREAT SCRIPTS

What separates an average puppet script from a great one? Some scripts fall all over themselves trying to be funny. Humor is a good thing, even an essential thing, but it needs to play a supporting role to the truth you're trying to teach.

A great puppet ministry script is based on a clear, simple Bible truth. And it doesn't stop with stating the truth—it shows the audience what it's like to live in the light of

the truth. A great script entertains and holds the audience's attention with winsome characters and appropriate touches of humor.

To write a great script, you'll need to focus on:

1. Plot
2. Story structure
3. Characterization

Let's get each of these elements working for you.

1. Plot

The plot is your story line: a conflict and a sequence of events that resolve it. Here are some sample conflicts that will pique the interest of every child in your ministry:

☺ Ashley and Becky were best friends—until Brittany moved to town. Becky started going to Brittany's house to play, and now Ashley feels rejected.

☺ A friendship is sorely tried when Jasper loses his watch. Kirby had asked to see it earlier in the day, so Jasper accuses him of taking it. But Kirby is innocent. How can he convince Jasper? Or can he?

☺ Jasper forgot to study for his test. He figures Kirby did, so he copies Kirby's answers, only to discover that Kirby didn't study either and made up all his answers! Now they'll both have the same wrong answers! Should Jasper save his neck by saying Kirby copied him, or tell the truth and get in bigger trouble?

☺ Jasper's mom goes out for the evening, leaving him with a babysitter who watches TV shows that are forbidden in Jasper's home. Should he take advantage of a chance to watch them?

☺ Keisha won't go to church camp because she's afraid of being away from her mom. Now the kids are calling her "Baby." What should she do?

Q: Why would kids be interested in these conflicts? (You don't get three guesses!)
A: Because they represent the sort of conflicts kids live out each day.

So as you think about stories for your puppets, make sure they're centered around issues that are important to kids. Here's a brief list of issues that kids confront as they mature and take responsibility for their actions and attitudes.

☺ Jealousy
☺ Covetousness
☺ Peer Pressure
☺ Conscience
☺ Safety
☺ Selfishness

- Patience
- Self control
- Justice
- Responsibility
- Faith
- Self esteem

You can add to this list very easily. Want to know how? Eavesdrop! Stand around the halls of your church and listen to what kids are talking about. It won't take long for you to catch on to what's important, troubling, funny and puzzling to your kids. Then you'll be able to develop scripts that meet real-life needs head-on. Your audiences will be eager to follow their puppet friends through the conflicts that bring about spiritual change.

The plot is a journey for your audience. By learning to be sensitive to their needs, you'll take them where they need to go.

2. Story Structure

You've studied your kids and you understand their needs. You've studied the Bible and God has guided you about how to address those needs. Now it's time to put the pieces of your story together. Don't worry if you're not a famous playwright. Skit writing is a skill you can learn.

Each skit needs:

- an exposition that sets the stage, introduces the characters and tells what they're doing.
- a conflict that challenges the characters.
- a resolution.

Since ministry skits are brief, you don't have time for long, drawn out expositions and complex character development. But with a little thought, you can establish characters and their situation with just a few well-crafted script lines. Here's an example.

MOM: Alright, Jasper. I'm going to Mrs. Goldberg's for awhile. Are you sure you'll be all right here by yourself?
JASPER: Yes, Mom! I'll be alright! I'm nine whole years old already! Gimme a break, will ya? [He sighs with disgust]

MOM: You watch your attitude, young man.

JASPER: Yes, ma'am.

MOM: Now, you can have anything you want for a snack today. And remember the rules of the house:

MOM and JASPER: "Don't use the stove, don't play with the appliances, and only watch the TV shows we allow here."

MOM: Can I trust you , Jasper?

JASPER: Yes, ma'am! You can trust me! [He turns to the audience and giggles nervously.]

This brief scene lets us know that Jasper is nine years old, and that he's being left at home alone for probably the first time. We can see that he is prone to attitude

problems, but that he basically respects his mother's authority. From the information in this brief exposition, you might correctly guess that the coming conflict has to do with the rules of the house. All of this takes just 30 seconds!

The next part of the skit should reveal a problem or conflict. In this case, a puppet who tempts Jasper is about to appear. He will try to persuade Jasper to use the

blender to make a milkshake—Jasper's favorite snack. Jasper can't see the tempter (even though the audience can), but he can hear the voice of temptation in his heart.

The climax needs to occur about 2/3 of the way into the skit. The milkshake skit reaches a climactic point when Jasper turns on the blender without the lid and the milkshake goes everywhere. (See Chapter 9 to learn how to make a safe splash that's easy to clean up.)

The last 1/3 of the skit presents the resolution and the lesson learned. Or, if you're doing a cliffhanger, you can leave your hero in the midst of the dilemma. In the case of the milkshake skit, Part 1 ends with Jasper being sent to his room. The second skit in the series shows Jasper being faced with a similar temptation, but choosing to obey his mom because of what he learned.

3. Characterization

Characters are so important! As you "give birth" to puppet characters, think carefully through their personalities. This is especially important when you're developing "starring" characters who will appear again and again.

Give each character a consistent personality. Is he cautious? Then don't let him slip up and say something impulsive. Is she sympathetic? Make sure her lines reflect a merciful, sympathetic attitude. Does he have a favorite funny expression? Drop it in from time to time.

Here's a handy character creation chart to get you started. Make as many photocopies of the chart as you need to for your own personal use. Why not take five minutes right now to begin creating the cast of your puppet productions? Have fun!

Answering these questions can help you enjoy your character and make her more interesting to others!

CHARACTER CREATION CHART

Name _____

Age_____ Temperament

Type of voice _____

Home or habitat _____

Hobbies/Interests _____

Family background _____

Good habits _____

Bad habits _____

Strengths _____

Weaknesses _____

Favorite cartoon/movie _____

Favorite colors _____

Favorite books _____

Favorite foods _____

Favorite expressions _____

Pets, Friends _____

Three "Potholes" of Scripting You Can Avoid

It's not hard to dodge these common potholes that leave scripts flat and stop the message dead in its tracks.

"CHURCHY" LANGUAGE

Speak properly, and in as few words as you can, but always plainly; for the end of speech is not ostentation, but to be understood.

William Penn

Choose plain English instead of "churchy" language. Stop and think: would someone who is visiting church for the first time understand what we're talking about, or is this a buzz word for the in-crowd at church? Here's an example of some perfectly well-intentioned language gone awry:

"Hi! Janie! Can't you just sense the presence of the Lord as we gather in his name? Hallelujah! I feel his touch in my life and my soul is bubbling over! Amen!"

Now try on this version, and see how much better it would feel to someone who's not familiar with the catch-phrases of church society.

"Hi, Janie! Doesn't it feel good to be here with other people who love God? It feels happy and safe! God is so neat! I can tell he's with me because I feel glad inside when I think about him! That must be what the pastor means when he says he's 'bubbling over with joy'!"

"Church speak" is fine among the initiated, but it really gets in the way with little ones and people who are new to church culture. And when these expressions are overused in church culture, they tend to hurt rather than help the cause of Christ because they sounds so stilted and other-worldly. Neither does it do any good when people use "amen" or "hallelujah" as casual, thoughtless fillers, in place of "um" or "uh". So don't let your puppets fall victim to the same disease. Here are examples of words and phrases to either avoid or use with caution as you create and edit puppet scripts.

Surely, verily, truly, victory, glory, amen, hallelujah, grace, saved, blessed, blessing, dwell in your heart, heavenly host, in my soul, sense in my spirit, covering, covenant, testimony, impart, righteous, holy, sanctified, anointing, brethren, presence, gift, thee, thou, giveth, taketh (in fact, all of the -eths and -ests), unto, hearken, Lamb of God, Lion of Judah, out of Egypt, in Zion, Canaan's land, inherit the land, take the land, uncircumcised, circumcised, delivered them into our hand, burden, travail, judgement, wrath, furnace of affliction, intercede, touch from the Lord, fiery trials,

With a little thought, you'll run across others. It's fine to introduce words that are common to the church crowd. Just make sure you explain them in dialog. Better yet, stick to plain English! It keeps your message fresh and accessible.

2. Blatant silliness

Giggles and fun are a good thing when they're in good balance with the rest of the script. Humor makes your scripts memorable and holds the kids' interest. Some puppeteers waste time with lots of obnoxious head-butting and screaming. Yuck! Keep a good balance.

CONVERSATION THAT GOES NOWHERE

Good scripts set up the situation and go straight for the heart of the conflict.

Meaningless conversation sometimes happens when puppeteers get stuck and don't know what else to say! Here's an example of meaningless puppet conversation:

MEL: Hey, Joe, how are you?

JOE: Fine, how are you?

MEL: Oh, not bad.

JOE: That's nice.

MEL: I'm glad that you think it's nice.

JOE: I do.

MEL: Oh. That's good.

JOE: Yeah.

MEL: What are you doin'?

JOE: Oh, nothin' much.

MEL: Nothin' huh? That's boring.

JOE: Yeah. I'm bored.

And so are we! How do you avoid a conversation that goes nowhere? At the very minimum, outline your script. Better yet, write it. Or use a prerecorded script.

It's not just amateur puppeteers who hit these potholes head-on. Evaluate scripts in the puppet books you purchase. If you see a pothole, patch it! Edit the undesirable part to make the script more compelling and worthwhile to your audience.

SIMPLE AND EFFECTIVE: MUSICAL SCRIPTS

Sometimes your puppets will be called on to fill a three to five-minute slot before a sermon or during the offering. In these cases, puppeteering to a recorded song may be just the right thing! If you're prefacing a sermon, you and the speaker can choose a song that will enhance the topic.

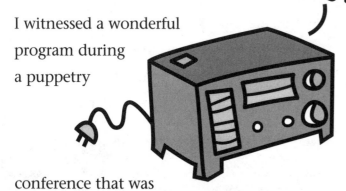

I witnessed a wonderful program during a puppetry conference that was built around the song, "Shut De Door, Keep out De Devil". The song had an African flavor, and the woman who directed this program (I regret not knowing her name) had built a set that resembled a jungle hut. Lights went out, a black light turned on,

So when you're on the spot for a quick, punchy performance, a song might just be the solution!

and a wonderful array of glow-in-the-dark creatures stepped out to sing. **The impact of this well-choreographed musical program has stayed with me for more than a decade!**

One of my personal puppet ministry highlights featured a troupe of 10 puppeteers between the ages of 7 and 12. We were asked to perform for the first time at a missionary conference before hundreds of people! Knowing that the kids were only weeks into their training, and months or years from mastering rod-arm puppet technique, I decided against a script. Instead, I opted for a song that could feature two or three of the children at a time in short appearances, then bring them all in for the last chorus.

Since I'm a writer/composer as well as puppeteer, I was able to create a recording of "God is So Good", using translations into 5 languages: French, a Chinese dialect, Spanish, Swahili, another African dialect, and English, with music styles conducive to each dialect. I made puppet costumes for each of those countries represented, and a few others just for spectacle. The resulting show was incredibly well received! The puppets popped up for their solos and duets. While the inexperience of the puppeteers had things a little out of sync, the arrangement of the song and the eye-catching costumes carried the performance. For the final verse of the song, all the puppets popped up out of a 3-level stage, forming an international puppet choir! The performance encouraged my 10 blossoming puppeteers and so engaged the audience that at the end, everyone was singing "God is so Good" with smiles on their faces.

So when you're on the spot for a quick, punchy performance, a song might just be the solution!

A FINAL WORD

Whatever script or song you choose, make sure it has substance. Kids don't need more empty, glitzy entertainment. They need entertainment that is brimming over with God's truth! Keep the sparkle, but add substance. Let your script pack as much practical, spiritual information as possible, always making sure the spectacle only serves to frame the message. Give the kids power for life—principles to hold in their hearts; principles to take home and apply to everyday situations. Give them God's word, by verse, or by example in puppet parables! Remember, the word of the Lord will not return void.

Puppet Show Today

chapter four

Recruiting Puppet People

Behind every great puppet is a great puppeteer who once upon a time knew nothing at all about puppetry.

HOW DO YOU GET VOLUNTEERS? Ask— and don't be shy. Your invitation can be the nudge that moves spectators into the exciting arena of service for God's Kingdom. Think of folks who are creative or have a flair for the dramatic, and ask if they'd like to help. Start with one or two helpers, learn a short skit and perform it during a church service. Follow it with a request for volunteers who'd like to operate a puppet or two and meet once a week at a set time for practice. You may get more than you expected!

THE HEART OF A VOLUNTEER

People who are honest-to-goodness puppeteers at heart (even though they may not know it yet!) will tend to display these qualities.

- *They're creative, but willing to take instruction from others.*
- *They have a good sense of rhythm (for lip-syncing) and timing.*
- *They're very expressive with puppets— maybe even more expressive than they are without them!*
- *Discipleship of kids is important to them.*

CHILDREN AS PUPPETEERS

If a polished puppet troupe is your goal, *target recruits who are 12 or older.* With the exception of a few specially gifted tykes, most children lack the discipline, endurance and skill to man a puppet correctly.

While your "A Level" troupe needs to be 12 and older, that doesn't mean there's no place for younger kids in your puppet ministry. If you have a group of children who are especially enthusiastic about getting involved with puppets, get them going with short weekly training sessions. Then give a special "puppet recital" where your puppeteers in training can perform a well-rehearsed skit or song before a live audience. Kids will love performing, and you'll have the beginnings of a great puppet troupe as they mature.

Of course, you want all your puppet characters to "survive" being handled by children. So begin your training by carefully reviewing guidelines for handling puppets. Set out your cast of puppet characters and go over the characteristics of each type of puppet. Photocopy and hand out "The 10 Commandments of Puppetry" found on page 38 at the end of this chapter. Use a puppet to teach and explain these important rules. Emphasize the fact that puppets are not toys, but ministry tools, and that handling them is a privilege.

Let younger kids begin by handling simple sock puppets. Better yet, let them make their own puppets! Turn to the puppet making ideas in Chapter X. Making their own puppets will give children ownership

of their training, and they'll come away with a tool to use in their own budding neighborhood puppet ministry! Kid who "graduate" from sock puppets can move on to more complex puppeteering.

TEENAGERS AS PUPPETEERS

Teenagers who are dedicated and enthusiastic about puppet ministry are some of the best puppeteers you'll ever find. They typically have the strength required to keep their arms up for long periods of time (you will come to understand the importance of this as you get going!), and the enthusiasm to bring their puppets to life.

Puppeteering is a great venue for teenagers who are normally a little shy about being up front. No worries about braces, skin

problems or self consciousness when a recorded script does the talking and all the live action is behind a stage! And even though puppet scripts are normally written for younger audiences, teenagers are far from immune from the truths they'll be teaching through puppets. What a great opportunity to get kids involved in discipleship and growing in their walk with God!

What you'll need to watch out for with teenage puppeteers is a tendency toward goofiness and overacting. The preventive for this is simply good training. "Stick to the script!" is great reminder to give kids before every performance.

ADULT PUPPETEERS

When an adult volunteers to be a puppeteer it's time to do the dance of joy! Why? Because an adult who is willing to give of his or her time and energy to be in puppet ministry is probably *called* to the role! With calling comes dedication—and you'll need troupe members who will stick with you through thick and thin. Someone with a van or truck may be "called to haul"! They can transport your stage and gear and help you set up and tear down. If God gives you such a person, you're a long way toward mastering some of the more challenging aspects of puppet ministry.

How Do You Recruit?

So how do you approach a potential volunteer for your puppet ministry team? There are a couple of ways to do this:

- Asking individually,
- Asking corporately.

It's not difficult to approach people, especially if you keep in mind that you're inviting them to step into a realm of service in God's kingdom that's fun and endlessly rewarding. You may know some creatively gifted people with drama backgrounds, or folks who are just plain animated! These energetic types are usually the first ones we think of, but don't forget the quiet types— they may surprise you with what they can do behind a curtain! I've known very shy people who became flamboyant Miss Piggy types with a puppet on their hand.

"Try on" these lead-ins and see which comes most naturally to you.

- "I've noticed the wonderful…you do. I'm building a puppet ministry team, and your gifts would fit in beautifully. Could I tell you about it?"
- "Have you seen the puppets perform in our church? We're looking for someone to… Would you consider helping out?
- May I see your hand? That's really amazing—I have a puppet that would fit

that hand just beautifully and I'd love to introduce you!

You don't just need puppet operators, remember. Depending on how extensive your ministry is going to be, you'll also need helpers to:

☾ Do carpentry work
☾ Do stage assembly
☾ Paint and decorate
☾ Haul equipment
☾ Buy costumes
☾ Sew costumes
☾ Make puppets
☾ Record scripts with character voices
☾ Run sound, lights and special effects

Many artistic people are just waiting for a chance to use their gifts for the Lord. If you know people who can take on these tasks, ask them if they'd like to be a vital part of a ministry that uses their God-given gifts!

When you ask, don't press the issue. Some very talented people just don't have the time or desire to participate in this kind of ministry, for whatever reasons. You don't have to ask "Why?" If the person declines, let them do so without guilt. If the best artist in the church declines to participate, don't feel she's being disobedient to God or

letting the church down. God will bring the right person to your aid—and it might just be yourself!

Many artistic people are just waiting for a chance to use their gifts for the Lord. If you know people who can take on these tasks, ask them if they'd like to be a vital part of a ministry that uses their God-given gifts!

Asking corporately gives a greater number of people a chance to respond—people you might not think of on your own. The very best way to ask a large group of people to participate in puppetry is to first give them a sample of what puppetry can do. Give them a show! Ask your pastor to give you a 5-minute slot in the Sunday morning service. It will help if you have one other person to operate a puppet. Rehearse the best skit you can find (Jasper and the Milkshake, at the end of this book, is always a crowd stopper.)

After performing your skit, ask the audience to consider participating by being a puppeteer, or by performing one of the other tasks listed above. Have a sign-up sheet available in the foyer and arrange for a meeting of volunteers at a set time and place. Call people who sign up to remind them of the meeting. When you have your meeting, be to tell them what is needed and how they can supply those needs in a specific way. Have a plan for when and where puppet ministry will take place— every week? At children's church only? On weeknights? Will you take the ministry to other churches, parks, fairs or festivals? People are more likely to make a commitment when they clearly understand your expectations.

SOME HELPS FOR YOU

The following two pages may be reproduced for use in your ministry. The first page shows "The Ten Commandments of Puppetry." This is a cute little piece to send home with each puppeteer. Stick one on the wall, and another on the inside of your puppet stage. Everyone who handles a puppet needs to know the rules. Your puppets will "live" longer that way!

The next reproducible is a flyer for new recruits. Photocopy the page and fill in the names and numbers of all recruits who sign up for puppet ministry. Also, fill in the rehearsal and meeting schedule blanks. Remember, the puppeteers will need to meet at least weekly to rehearse. But others, such as haulers and set-up persons may need to meet only before a major production. Art people and set builders want to meet regularly until sets are built and painted. Then they may have a month or more off until you need more props or sets. These artists may be able to arrange their own meeting times. For example, all of the set designers may be able to meet during the day while kids are in school. If you aren't one of the art people, delegate someone to head this up. That person can schedule all artists and builders while you train the puppeteers. Let your volunteers have as much autonomy as is practical.

The key to unity is having a single purpose— to put on a great program with a Christian message. Resist the temptation to focus on showcasing your talent and being admired. Stay in the shadows. Let Christ be magnified!

The Ten Commandments of Puppet Care

1. Thou shalt not use thy puppet as a boxing glove.

2. Thou shalt not hold thy puppet by its nose, ear, eyelash, tongue, button or any other protrusion that could come loose over time.

3. Thou shalt not allow thy puppet to touch the floor or any other potentially dirty surface.

4. Thou shalt not leave thy puppet in direct sunlight or in a hot car, as many can fade, warp and bend thereby.

5. Thou shalt not touch thy puppet with sticky or dirty hands, nuzzle thy puppet while wearing makeup, or kiss thy puppet while wearing lipstick, lip gloss or other goo.

6. Thou shalt not use thy puppet's mouth to bite other puppets, pinch people, or to pick up thine items.

7. Thou shalt not store thy puppets in such a way that they could become wrinkled, crimped, squashed or bent.

8. Thou shalt keep thy puppet's hair combed and clothing pressed.

9. Thou shalt clean thy puppet only in the way prescribed for its fabric and decorative components.

10. Thou shalt put thy puppet in its proper place after use.

Welcome to our Puppet Ministry!

Congratulations—you're about to fulfill a very special calling!
Thanks to you many children and adults will hear the Gospel
in a way that's entertaining and rich in Bible truth!
Here's a list of all the wonderful people on our staff.

NAME ....

PHONE ....

EMAIL ....

NAME ....

PHONE ....

EMAIL ....

NAME ....

PHONE ....

EMAIL ....

NAME ....

PHONE ....

EMAIL ....

NAME ....

PHONE ....

EMAIL ....

**PUPPET MINISTRY MEETINGS
WILL BE HELD AS FOLLOWS:**

Puppeteers

Day ....

Time ....

Location ....

Set designers, builders, costumers, puppet makers, technicians

Day ....

Time ....

Location ....

Call or email me with any questions or concerns.

Name ....

Email ....

Work Phone ....

Home Phone ....

chapter **five** # Tricks of the Trade

Success is not final, failure is not fatal: it is the courage to continue that counts. —Sir Winston Churchill

A CHARMING LITTLE FIGURE MADE OF FELT or fur lies on the shelf of your closet. It's inert and lifeless—just fabric and plastic. You slip your hand inside the body and wiggle your fingers into the mouth. It turns its little head to look at you, the mouth starts to move, and through the marvelous avenue of imagination, you give the little figure a voice, a personality, awareness and feelings. What a wonderful moment!

Those are the moments you're working to build when you use puppets to interact with children and teach them important truths from God's Word. When you use puppets in God's ministry, you want to do it with every skill you can bring to bear. Maybe you've have some experience with puppets. Or perhaps you're picking up a

puppet for the first time. Either way, you'll find this chapter a real treat.

PUPPETEER TYPES

First, let's look at the puppeteer types. Almost everybody will fall into one of the following funny categories, so don't worry when you see yourself or every one of your puppeteers' foibles described! The purpose of this section is not to discourage you, but to make you aware that not every willing heart is going to have a skillful hand to go with it in the beginning. It's normal to go through these phases as you start your ministry. Some very energetic people jump right in, never realizing their funny little foibles until they see themselves on video! Here are a few examples we've encountered:

THE "UNSYNC-ABLE" MOLLY BROWN

The Molly Browns are the folks just can't get the hang of synchronizing a puppet's mouth to spoken words! These are the dear ones whose puppets' mouths will be closed on a vowel sound and open when they're humming! Watching them perform is like watching an Italian movie—without subtitles!

THE SHRINKER

Shrinkers are those who can't seem to keep the puppet upright during the program. This is not always a matter of strength, but a matter of spatial perspective. Some puppeteers need help gauging the height of the  puppet curtain from below, so they'll know whether their puppet is standing waist-high, neck-high, or whether—oh, no!—their own arm is showing! Conquering this problem is a matter of practice. Sometimes videotaping rehearsals can help puppeteers gauge the height of their puppets.

THE BIRDWATCHER

Birdwatchers have trouble holding the puppet's head down because they fail to bend their wrists at a proper angle. As a result, the puppet's face points upward and the audience sees the puppet's chin and throat area instead of the face. It is very distracting, especially to children who start looking upward to see what's so special about the ceiling...

THE HEAD POPPER

Head Poppers are those whose puppets heads pop backward every time they speak. This happens when the puppeteer uses the fingers to lift the mouth open instead of pulling the thumb downward to work the lower jaw.

YOUR FIX-IT KIT

Almost every person who enters puppetry starts out with one of the challenges listed above. The good news is that most puppeteers are trainable, and this guide can help.

Every good puppeteer has a mental "toolbox" packed with tips of the trade that bring the those endearing little bundles of fabric and fur to life. Here's your toolbox! With a little focused practice, you and your puppet troupe can whiz right by "mediocre" all the way to "marvelous"!

As with most manual skills, the key is practice. Oh, no! Your mother has been telling you that since you started piano lessons when you were seven years old! Well, your mother was right. But with puppetry it doesn't take a lifetime. You can be presenting programs with real pizzazz in just a few weeks. So let's dig in to that tool box, starting with the top three essential skills.

TOOL #1: PUPPET POSTURE

The first element in powerful puppetry is posture. Believe it or not, puppets can slump and slouch and gawk and even be too stiff. Some of these postures are called for in certain characters or situations. But most of the time you'll want your puppets to appear to stand naturally. Grab a puppet and work through each of these steps. You'll be amazed at how much you can accomplish in just a few minutes!

Height

Make sure your puppet is high enough to be seen. This is harder than it seems, especially if you are using a large, relatively heavy puppet. The puppeteer who falls into the "Shrinker" category will gradually lose arm strength or focus. Meanwhile, the audience sees the puppet sink to shoulder height, then perhaps lean slightly, and keep shrinking until he drops out of sight. The cure for this is practice and weight lifting.

Every puppeteer has his or her own preferred stance during a performance. You may choose to kneel on a padded gardening mat as you operate your puppets. If that sounds a little like torture, then a swivel chair might be the right choice for you. One caveat with a chair: remember to keep your head down. Seeing a tuft of hair appear above the stage floor may bring a chuckle from the audience, but it can also destroy the flow of the show. So practice being a "sitting duck"!

Practice keeping your puppet at just the right height so none of your arm shows. A good puppeteer is the model of modesty— nothing shows at all! Keeping yourself completely out of sight maintains the important illusion that you're not there, and that the puppet you're operating doesn't "morph" into you behind the curtain. If you surprise the audience with a peek at your arm, think of the potential shock when they realize that your puppet has no body from the waist down!

Practice correct puppet height with a partner, or set up a video camera and tape yourself.

Stance

Some beginner puppeteers have trouble keeping their puppets' backs straight. In the effort to keep the puppet high enough, you may tend to lean to one side and your

WRONG

puppet may look like the Leaning Tower of Pisa! Other puppeteers, weary from keeping their arms upright, rest their puppets' tummies on the front bar of the PVC stage. This not only makes the puppet look ill as he sways over the bar—

you risk toppling your stage if you put too much weight on the stage! This actually happened during one of my

RIGHT

programs. The pipe was not properly secured and it fell apart, pipe by pipe, releasing the sceneboard, and revealing two mortified puppeteers still sitting in their chairs like a couple of Rahabs at Jericho!

No matter what your stage is made of, it you can damage or topple it by leaning. Yes, your arms can get tired. Think of it as physical workout. All these ministry benefits and weight training too! Besides gaining upper body strength, you'll make sure cardboard doesn't bend, sheets don't fall, ropes don't give way and boards don't tumble. Good puppet posture is also your best calamity prevention program.

As you work with other puppeteers, make it a rule not to lean on the stage. That's sissy stuff!

Head

The "Birdwatcher's" common mistake in puppet operation is to point the face too far upward, giving the audience a view of the puppet's

WRONG

throat and chin instead of the mouth and eyes.   The cure for this is to train yourself to bend your hand downward at the wrist. While you don't want your puppet looking at the ground, you do want your audience to see its face.

Remember that the eye level for your audience is usually lower than for your puppets—especially when children are sitting on the floor. Pointing the head slightly downward will give everyone a better view. And this is most important if your puppet is talking to the audience. You want the puppet to be addressing the audience, not the lighting system!

Tool #2: Mouths in Motion

Convincing puppetry is always based on mouths in motion. Getting your puppet's mouth the synchronize the with words is one of the most important skills for you to conquer. There are just a couple of simple principles to follow. After that, all you need is a bit of practice.

If your puppet is saying "Marvelous!", open the mouth with each vowel sound and close it with each consonant. For many people, this comes quite naturally. For others (the "Unsync-able Molly Browns"), it's a struggle to keep from clamping down on the vowels. But even the most stubborn Mollies can learn to do it correctly with practice. M-ar-v-e-l-ou-s!

AH

EH

CONSONANT

AN OPEN AND SHUT CASE

When people speak, their lower jaws move as they form words. Puppets should do the same. When they don't, the puppet's head pops back with a jerk with each vowel sound. Imagine a vise holding your lower jaw still while saying "Dynamite!" Your upper jaw would take over and your entire head would move backward! This is exactly what "Head-poppers" do with their puppets. This action is irritating to viewers, and needs to be tamed. Here's how.

Instead of opening the mouth by simply spreading the space between your thumb and fingers, open the mouth by pulling your thumb downward. This isn't an easy or natural action. The muscles that pull the thumb downward are usually not as strong as those that spread the thumb and forefinger. So you'll need to develop those weaker muscles through practice.

While you're learning to pull your thumb down, use this little trick. When you open the mouth, jut the puppet's head downward slightly in kind of a spiking motion. Over-spiking or scooping will look goofy, but if you practice in front of a mirror, you'll soon come up with a workable style. And your puppets will be safe from upper jaw whiplash!

TOOL #3 WELL ARMED!

Rod-arm puppets can move both arms while speaking. It takes a bit of coordination, but you'll get there.

Wear the puppet on one hand and hold the two rods with the other. People have different ways of holding the rods to maneuver them together, just as people hold chopsticks and crochet hooks in different ways. Rather than trying to impose a "correct" way upon you and your team, experiment until you find your most comfortable method. A good starting point is to cross the rods scissors-style. Move the arms together—perhaps to the rhythm of a song. That's stage one.

When you're ready, move on to holding the rods together about four inches from the bottom so you can "pinch" them and make your puppet clap its hands. If you can make your puppet applaud without looking like a slo-mo video clip, you're on your way to mastering the rods! (Hot tip: use your rod arm practice as an excuse to go out for Oriental food so you can eat with chopsticks and increase your coordination!)

Once you get into the groove with the rod arms, don't feel compelled to use BOTH rods all the time. It's a lot of work and it looks unnatural. People don't always use both hands at once; neither should your puppet—he's an anthropomorph, after all.

Try dropping one of the rods and using the other to scratch the head. Now pick up the other rod (so that you have two) and put both hands out, pleadingly. Then drop the puppet's hands to the side, face his head downward, and have him walk away. See how dramatic that little segment can be? Try it over and over, inventing words he might say while moving his arms. After a while, it will come to you so naturally you won't even think about it—much like learning to type.

NOW FOR DESSERT

When you master posture and moving mouths and arms, you can put together a convincing puppet performance. But why stop there? Take on the challenge of these moves to attain real puppeteering excellence.

TOOL #4: WALKING YOUR PUPPET

Unless she's Michelle Kwan gliding in on skates, your puppet is going to bounce a bit when she enters or exits. And unless you have a door for her to enter and exit through, she's going to enter from below the stage. Don't have her just pop up like a Jack-in-the-box out of the floor. Have her lightly bounce up from one side, as if she's climbing stairs. When she walks around your set, have her bounce slightly, as if she really had jointed, working legs.

TOOL #5: OPENING DOORS

Watching a puppet open a door can be a lot of fun for audiences, so this skill is worth the extra practice it takes. When your puppet approaches the door, use one rod to lift a hand to the doorknob. Use the hand that is holding the rod to pull open the door while keeping the puppet's hand on the knob. While it looks clumsy to you, the maneuver looks smooth and sophisticated to the audience.

TOOL #6: TURNING AROUND

If you want your puppet to make a complete 360° turn, you need to either be on your knees on a swivel chair, stool or backless chair. Try it in a regular chair and find out why! And don't forget, when you move the puppet around, allow him to bob a little, as if he is taking steps with real little legs and feet. People don't turn around without bobbing, so neither should your puppet.

TOOL #7: SHOWING EXPRESSION

Most puppets have stationary eyes, eyebrows, mouths and cheeks, so expression has to be done with the whole body. Try these ideas.

Surprise: Wear the puppet on one hand, hold the bottom of its body with the other. Now, in one movement, open his mouth while pulling his head down—without moving his shoulders.

Sadness: Leave arm rods dangling. Point the puppet's face downward, mouth closed, and roll the head slightly (and slowly) side to side in a figure 8 by pressing down alternately with the index finger, then the pinkie.

Joy: Bounce the puppet up and down while clapping his hands with the rods.

Fear: Keep the puppet's mouth slightly open and quiver while holding the puppet's hands to its chest or mouth.

If you're training a team of new puppeteers, choose two or three "tools" to practice each week. Critique each other. You'll stay on top of the encouragement curve if you start by performing to a simple song. Introduce the more complex moves slowly. It's really tempting to go for all the bells and whistles, but resist! Build your skills gradually. Your audiences will be delighted and surprised as you add sophistication to your performances over time.

chapter six

Dress Up and Set the Stage

*C*lothes make the man. — Latin Proverb

IF YOU'RE LIMITED IN THE NUMBER OF PUPPETS you can afford (and who isn't), you might opt for a couple of hairless puppets and a gorgeous wardrobe from the local second-hand store!

I use a single bald puppet named Jean-Luc to play more than five different roles: Jasper's mom; 12-year-old Becky; a middle-aged bespectacled teacher named Mr. Severe; an elderly white-haired woman; and a variety of extras. All it took was some smart shopping at yard sales and used clothing stores.

For example, I bought every wig I could get my hands on—gray hair, blonde hair, brown, black, curly, straight, whatever, for about a dollar each. Some of the wigs fit Jean-Luc perfectly. Others fit by taking in a couple of side seams. And some of the gray wigs made terrific beard/mustache combos with a little careful cutting. These were affixed to the puppet with safety pins to allow for swift changes between scenes.

Large-size puppets have bodies about the size of a 6- to 12-month-old baby. This means you can go to your local second-hand shop and find turtleneck shirts, sweatshirts, cardigans and tees in 12-month sizes that will just fit! The key is to buy colors, patterns and styles that do not look like baby clothes. For example, I came across a burgundy collegiate sweatshirt from Harvard in size 12 months! This became one of Jasper's favorite shirts, but it could also have been used for a college student in a campus ministry skit.

If you make your own bald puppet for the purpose of using it for multiple characters, make it with Velcro® tabs instead of eyes. That way, you can make different sets of eyes with Velcro® tabs in the back. Girl puppets can even have long eyelashes attached.

Here are some tips for dressing your puppets to create a variety of characters.

Granny

For a female senior citizen, start with a gray or white wig. If you can't find one, make one out of white faux fur. Put a little topknot of white fur on the top for a bun.

A pair of glasses will help the look, especially if you can find a pair of wire frames or horn-rimmed glasses. Many dollar stores sell sunglasses for children and adults. Buy a pair and poke out the lenses and you have a pair of glasses for your granny puppet.

She'll feel comfy in a baby girl's button-up blouse with a plain cardigan sweater over it. Button the sweater and let the blouse collar show. Add a brooch or string of pearls and she's ready for a nice cup of tea!

Bald Man

If you're working with a hairless puppet, the head is all set. Or, you can give him a different kind of bald head by cutting a strip of faux fur to fit around his head, 2-inches wide. Make sure to cut the strip so that the nap of the fur runs with the width and not the length. Round the edges and pin it around his head. In just a snap you've given him a nice chrome-dome with a tasteful circle of hair. Quite distinguished!

If the man is to be a teacher or businessman, you might add black-rimmed

glasses. For a shirt, use a little boy's white dress shirt—as small as you can find. You may have to use a toddler size. The length of the shirt tail won't matter, since it will be out of sight, but you may need to roll up the sleeves a bit. Find a little boy's clip-on tie, and your puppet will take on a very adult look.

If possible, find a very small suit coat. You'll be amazed at what a little suit coat does for a puppet in a shirt and tie! Your puppet will become a little man!

Little Boy

This is an easy puppet to dress. It's a snap to find striped polo shirts, sweatshirts and other little-boy clothing in 9-12-month sizes. Stay away from baby pastels. Look for shirts in primary colors—red, yellow, green, blue. Black and brown are bonus colors for shirts, if you can find them.

Baby boy baseball caps—even those with logos on them—are great for little boys! Have your puppet wear a cap frontward or backward, depending on his character. If it's a plain hat, you can personalize it with fabric puff paint! In fact, you can write your puppet's name on his sweatshirt, too.

Little Girl

Little girls are fun to dress up. Start by finding some non-baby-looking baby girl clothes, such as sweatshirts, crew-necks, turtlenecks and tees. A number of wig types can be used for little girls. You can also make one from faux fur, and put pigtails on each side using a "tube" of fur sewn to each side. Finish them off with pretty ribbons, scrunchies or barrettes. You might want to buy some false eyelashes to affix to the eyes. Make your little girl puppet as current and fashionable as

possible. Kids will relate to a cool-looking puppet, so be on the looking for what's "in" with the kids in your ministry group.

Mother

Mothers can wear a variety of shirts and sweaters, depending on whether she's going to work or baking cookies in the kitchen. The important thing is the hair. A curly wig is perfect for Mom. Earrings are an option that adds a bit of age in most cases. Hook earrings work well—all you have to do is stick the hook into the fabric where the ear should be.

CLOTHING ITEMS TO LOOK FOR

When you're cruising the garage sales or visiting your local second hand store, look for the following items in infant and toddler sizes for creating interesting characters and extras:

- Baseball caps
- Other hats
- Denim jackets
- Suit coats
- Cardigan sweaters
- Non-pastel colored shirts
- Boy's white dress shirts
- Girls headbands and hair accessories
- Wigs
- Jewelry
- Eyeglasses, sunglasses
- Parkas, jackets
- Sweatshirts with or without logos and icons

Now you have a great excuse to go garage sale-ing! If shopping around for "second hand Rose" treasures isn't your favorite thing, you probably know someone who loves to do just that. Alert moms in your congregation that you can use clothes that their little ones outgrow. You'll be surprised at how quickly your wardrobe closet grows.

And don't think you need to take all of the burden on yourself. Enlist the help of crafters in your congregation. Those who sew, knit, crochet and make dolls would probably be delighted to have an invitation from you to be your chief wardrobe designer.

You can put things on a puppet that you would never dream of putting on yourself. So have fun!

STAGING

You've got your puppets adorably dressed. Now it's time to set the stage! This chapter will give you lots of options for staging. You can go from simple to elaborate, depending on the style of show you produce and the resources you have available.

In a pinch, you can drape a sheet from chair to chair, or cut a window from an appliance box. It's quite simple (really!) to build a portable theatre with PVC pipe. You can even purchase professional lighting stands. If you integrate puppets with humans in drama, puppets can sit on windowsills, tabletops, trees, and other places where the puppeteers can easily be hidden. In some cases, you may want to carry a puppet on your arm with no stage at all! There are ways to do this without giving away your identity as puppeteer.

Sheet Curtains

Who hasn't set up a backyard stage with a sheet and a clothesline? Sheets are primitive, but can work in a pinch—

especially on mission trips to remote locations where a stage is impractical. Just run a rope through the top fold-over hem of a sheet and stretch the rope between two objects, about 4-1/2 feet off the ground. Voilà! You are ready to perform!

Cardboard Box Stages

Don't laugh—refrigerator boxes can be very effective, especially when only you're only using one puppet. The box can be custom decorated according to the needs of your presentation. For example, if the puppet is a bird or squirrel, the box can become a big, hollow tree. All you need is a little imagination and a free evening. This task is ideal for a small group of teens or creative adults, so consider the possibilities for fun and fellowship!

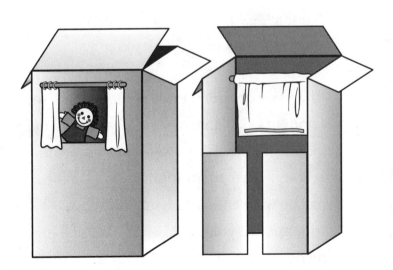

A Hollow Tree Art

You might want to create this tree in its permanent location, as it may not be very portable when you're finished. First, cut a hole in the front of the box for the puppet, and an entry hole or door in the back for the puppeteer. Be sure the puppet's hole is high enough to obscure the puppeteer's entry hole as well as the puppeteer. Cut off the top and bottom of the box and bend it into an upright "tunnel", rounding the corners as much as possible. Don't worry about the "wrinkles"—in fact, vertical wrinkles will add to the look of bark.

When you get the roundness you desire, set it upright on a large piece of plywood, vinyl flooring, or anything else you can spare to serve as a permanent foundation (4' x 4' may be wide enough). Using duct tape strips applied vertically, secure the tube to the floorboard all the way around. Neatness does not count here as you will soon see.

Crumple newspaper into balls and tape them together to form "roots" at the base of the tree (These will be covered by papier mache.). The roots should be largest at the base, narrowing out on the floorboard. Leave big spaces between each root for a realistic look.

Now the fun begins. Tear long strips of old cotton cloth or newspaper, about 4 inches wide. (Cloth is best, but use what you have.) Dip the strips in papier mache mixture (see the recipe on page xx) and affix them VERTICALLY to the cardboard trunk. Don't be afraid to pinch the wet strips vertically to create a rough bark texture. Cover the roots with papier mache as well, blending them into the floorboard. This will need to dry overnight—possibly longer.

For branches, use crumpled newspaper balls taped together to form narrowing branches. Duct-tape them high on the tree trunk. If the branches are too long to stand up, brace them to the tree with a stick (from a real tree) running from the branch diagonally upward to the trunk so it looks like a stray branch or vine. Tape in place, and papier mache the new branches to the tree.

After they dry for a day or so, paint the tree. For the trunk, use charcoal gray paint with a tinge of brown. This is more realistic than plain brown. When the paint is dry, dip a large brush or sponge dipped in white, light gray or beige paint, and remove all excess so that the brush is quite dry. Starting in the back (in case you mess up), gently brush over the rough bark with this highlighting color and watch the texture appear!

Cut out green tissue paper leaves in various shades and tape them all over the branches and trunk.

So much for the idea that cardboard box puppet stages are inferior!

The Television Set

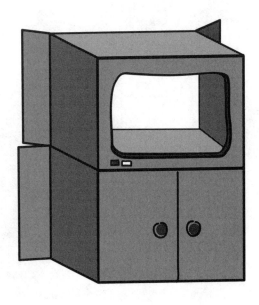

Having puppets appear in a TV set is a great way to do monologues or short skits with only a couple of characters. One refrigerator box or two smaller boxes (an appliance box with a TV-sized box) can make a great TV stage!

If you're using the refrigerator box, start by closing all flaps and securing them with packing tape. On what will be the front of the TV stage, measure and draw a TV screen on the top 1/3 of the box. Leave a 2-inch "frame" around the screen. Use a box cutter to carefully excise the screen from the box. Go to the back of the stage and measure a door on the bottom half of the box. You may choose to cut out the entire door, or cut a capital "I" to create double doors. The double doors can be bent back to help support the stage.

Once you've done the cutting, it's time to decorate! You may paint the TV frame and sides with black paint. Draw a straight line across the box, about 5 inches below the screen area and add control buttons.

The entire lower 2/3 of the box can be painted to look like a TV stand or piece of furniture. Choose any color you'd like.

You may use this TV as is, or for a really cool TV effect, you may easily create a realistic TV screen with cheesecloth and in-box lighting. Cut a piece of theatre muslin to cover the screen hole from the inside. Use a hot glue gun to adhere the cloth to the box. Make sure it's stretched tightly.

Next, hang a string of white Christmas lights around the inside of the screen. Go around two or three times if the light string is long enough. Just make sure the string is duct-taped securely to the cardboard.

The lights are not to be seen from the outside. The purpose of the lights is to illuminate the front of the puppet from the inside so that he will not be in the shadows. When the TV is "on" (the lights), the puppet can be almost magically seen through the screen. When the TV is "off," the screen will appear opaque, and your puppet will not appear! This makes entering and exiting a breeze! All you need is a responsible team member to man the light switch!

PVC Pipe Stage (portable)

The PVC pipe stage is one of the most practical of all puppet stages. It can be constructed of ordinary plumbers' PVC pipe, with curtains made of wrinkle-free polyester fabric or dark, solid-color bed sheets. Once you get the hang of it, you can assemble and tear down this stage in just a few minutes. And the stage can support elaborate plywood sceneboards held in place with hooks and bungee cords from the back.

This is such a great stage that I know you'll want to make it! You'll find detailed assembly instructions in Chapter 7.

Theatre Flats Art

Flats are the pieces of stagecraft that form walls and other parts of a professional theatre set. Each flat consists of a wood frame measuring 8 ft. tall and 4 ft. wide (made of 2 by 4s). The flat is covered with "theatre muslin", a coarse, inexpensive cotton fabric found in almost any fabric store. The muslin is stretched and stapled over the frame, then "painted" with a mixture of white glue and water. When the muslin dries, it stretches tightly, forming a smooth surface for painting.

When a puppet needs to sit on a windowsill, in a tree painted on the flat, etc., you'll want to make the flat from lightweight plywood and cover it with muslin. Cut the hole wherever you need it. Then paint all your flats to match.

Finger Puppet Theatre

This little cereal-box theatre is also featured in <u>FUNtastic KidCrafts</u> (by the author). It's easy enough for a child to make! It provides a wonderful little stage for the tiniest of puppets, and it has a real curtain you can raise and lower with the turn of a knob!

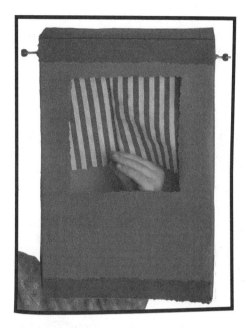

Materials:

9 oz. - 14.5 oz. cereal box
Ruler
Scissors
Construction paper
Glue
Washable markers
Skewer
Pony beads
Piece of fabric about the size of the front of the box

Directions:

Remove the top from the cereal box.
Turn the box upside down and draw a large rectangle on the front, leaving two inches at the top, 1-1/2 inches at the sides, and at least five inches at the bottom (the open end). Cut out the square.
Cover the box with construction paper.

Cut the fabric so it's wider than the hole in the box, and a couple of inches longer. Glue the top edge of the fabric around the skewer.

Poke two small holes in the sides of the box, only an inch from the top, and 1/2-inch from the front. From inside the box, stick the two ends of the skewer—it's a curtain for your stage.

Glue pony beads to each end of the skewer to cover sharp points and to keep the skewer from slipping out either side. Roll the skewer to raise and lower the curtain. Draw faces on your fingers with washable marker and let them put on a show!

Or…No Stage At All!

If you opt for adding legs to your puppet, or if you can "hide" her in a blanket or other prop, you can just walk around and talk to the kids, one on one! A portable puppet is a great help when you're asking questions and want to encouraging group participation.

chapter seven Building a PVC-Pipe Stage

*"**B**y perseverance the snail reached the ark."*
— Charles Haddon Spurgeon

PERHAPS YOU'VE TURNED TO THIS CHAPTER with a dubious frown. "I'm not a carpenter or a construction engineer," you're thinking. "No way am I going to tackle stage construction." Well, guess what. *You can do this!* PVC pipe is inexpensive, readily available, light weight and easy to cut with a hacksaw. In fact, when I built my first stage, I actually cut the PVC pipe with an old bread knife!

We'll walk you through the process step-by-step with pictures and detailed instructions. So get ready for your trip to the home improvement store.

For a stage that's 6 ft. wide, 7.5 ft. high (at the highest point), and 6 ft. deep, you'll need:

- ❧ 2-inch PVC pipe in the following lengths:
    - 2.5 ft. (8 pieces)
    - 2 ft. 9 in. (8 pieces)
    - 3.5 ft. (6 pieces)
    - 4.5 ft. (6 pieces)
    - 6 ft. (3 pieces)
    - 7 ft. 3 in. (1 piece)

- ☙ 2-inch PVC joints as follows:
    - 4-way crosses (2)
    - 3-way elbows (10)
    - 3-way tees (6)

- ☙ Small can of PVC cement
- ☙ Rubber tape in 4 colors (black, red, blue and green)
- ☙ Black permanent marker
- ☙ Wrinkle-resistant, non-shrinkable fabric
- ☙ Color-matched thread
- ☙ Optional but helpful: Bungee cords in varied lengths

Directions:

Get off on the right foot by marking each piece of PVC pipe before you begin to assemble it. The color coding is a real time saver!

Mark the following PVC pieces with rings of black tape about 5 inches from each end:

Four—2.5 ft. pieces
Two—2 ft. 9 in. pieces

Mark the following PVC pieces with rings of red tape about 5 inches from each end:
All six 4.5 ft. pieces
Four 2 ft. 9 in. pieces
The 7 ft., 3 in. piece

Mark the following PVC pieces with rings of blue tape about 5 inches from each end:
One 6-ft. piece
Four 2.5 ft. pieces

Mark the following PVC pieces with rings of green tape about 5 inches from each end:
One 6-ft. piece
Two 3.5 ft. pieces
Two 2 ft. 9 in. pieces

BLACK PIECES:

The black pieces will create a rectangle that will serve as the base of your stage.

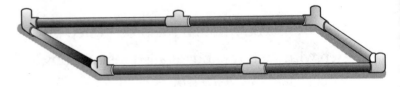

The other pieces will connect to this base, so align them accordingly.

Using PVC cement, glue two of the 2.5 ft. pieces together lengthwise, with a 3-way tee between them. Push the pipe all the way in. You may need to use a rubber mallet for this. Repeat for the other two pieces.

In the same way, glue the two 2 ft. 9 in. pieces together with a 3-way tee between them. Glue a 3-way elbow on one end of this new piece for a corner connection. Make sure the center "tube" of the elbow is facing the same direction as the open tube of the tee the was glued in the center of the pipe.

Glue a 3-way elbow on each end of the 6 ft. piece as you did above, again making sure the open ends of the elbows are facing the same directions (parallel). If these open ends are not perfectly parallel, your stage will be crooked when you put it together.

RED PIECES:

Take a 4.5 ft. piece and glue a 4-way tee joint to one end. Glue a 2 ft. 9 in. piece of pipe to the tee joint, creating a pipe about 7 ft. 3 in. long. Make another piece just like it. Then make two more, using 3-way tees instead of 4-way tees.

BLUE PIECES

Glue 3-way elbows to both ends of the 6 ft. piece, making sure the open ends are aligned to face the same way.

GREEN PIECES

Glue a 3-way elbow to both ends of the 6-ft. green piece, like the blue piece you just finished.

Glue the two 2 ft. 9 in. pieces together with a 3-way tee, forming a 6 ft. pipe with a joint in the middle.

Congratulations! You just finished creating your puppet frame components. Now it's time to put it all together.

ASSEMBLY

First, lay the black pieces on the floor using the 6 ft. piece with the center joint as the back of your base. Connect the two slightly shorter pieces to the floor-side end joints. They should be running parallel, away from the back. Connect the remaining black piece to the parallel pipes so that the remaining open join ends of this piece point upward.

The order of assembly you choose for the rest of the stage may depend on the help

you have available. The following is suitable for two persons working parallel on the sides of the stage. It will help to round up the pieces for each side ahead of time so they're within reach as you put things together.

Begin by attaching some of the red and blue pieces. First, place the two short red pieces into the open joint ends of the base front. Take the 6 ft. blue piece and attach it to the tops of the red pieces and press them in tightly.

While you hold this frame upright, grab the 2.5 ft. (short) pieces and insert them into the open joints at the top so that they face toward the back. While you're holding these up, pick up the tall red pieces with the 4-way tees and insert them into the center joints on the sides of the base. Then insert the other end of the blue piece into the center tee. Now it should stand on its own.

Place the long, uninterrupted green pipe on top of the tall red pipes, so that the open joints of the green pipe face side to side, and

backward. Press in securely. Next, take the two 3 ft.-3 in. blue pipes and insert them into the remaining receptacles of the four-way tees, facing the back. Reach down and grab the tall red pipes with the 3-way tees, and insert them into the back of the base, long end down. Attach the remaining blue pipes in the open joints that face each other.

Attach the long green pipe (with the center tee) to the tops of the tall red pipes. Attach the short green pipes to the remaining sides, and your stage frame is complete! For added strength, wrap bungee cords horizontally around the side pipes.

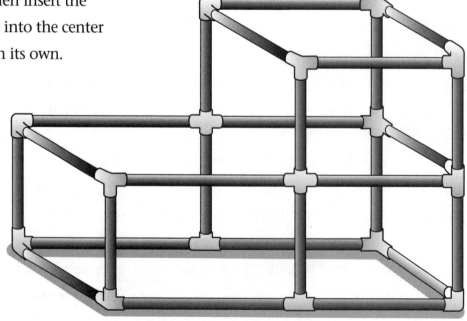

CURTAINS

Now your stage is ready to be draped. These guidelines are for beginners, but sewing experts can combine these basics with their own ideas for even better results!

Curtains need to be made of dark, solid fabric. Black is best if you're going to do any black light performances (see Chapter 9 on special effects for details about this exciting option!) Choose a durable, washable, opaque fabric that resists wrinkling. Sometimes you can find inexpensive, wrinkle-resistant bed sheets that can be cut and sewn into curtains. Navy blue works pretty well. Make sure you buy enough of one dye lot to finish the project.

Measure each panel area of the stage separately, A through F.

"Gathered" curtains can be made by measuring the width of each panel (the space between pipes) and doubling it. For a less gathered look, don't double the width of each panel, but increase it by half. For no gathering at all, just add a few inches to the width of each panel for seams and basting the edges. But keep in mind that gathering hides the seams—and most wrinkles.

Panel A

45-in. width fabric: Measure 3 pieces, 66 inches in length. Lay two pieces with the right sides together, matching length and width. Stitch a seam down one of the long sides. Open the pieces, right side up. Place the remaining piece right side down and match the edges with one of the sides of the larger piece. Stitch a seam down the long edge so that you form a 3-paneled piece.

Open the seams and press neatly. Baste or hem-stitch all the way around.

Now, using a needle and matching thread, attach Velcro® tabs (the rough half) on the wrong side, just under the top edge. Place them evenly, every four to six inches, all the way across the curtain. Next, fold the tabbed edge over about 9 inches (be sure you can loosely wrap it around a piece of PVC pipe. Using a piece of chalk, mark where the Velcro® tabs meet the wrong side of the curtain. Place the matching Velcro® tabs (soft half) on the chalk marks and stitch neatly, knowing the stitches will show on the right side.

Now you can hang your drape over the front pipe of the stage and press the tabs in place. Once it's hung, pin the bottom for the hem. Make sure the hem touches the floor. It can even be a little longer to make sure nothing under your stage will ever show.

Panels B through F

Repeat this process of measuring, cutting and stitching for the remaining panels. (note: Panel B should hang 6 inches below the front pipe of panel A).

You will need to place matching Velcro® tabs between the panels (you can decide how many are needed), to make sure nothing inside the stage will show. Position

these tabs with some fabric overlap to close all holes. Panels closest to the front should always be on top, working your way to the back.

Corners

You'll notice right away that the PVC corners show. Corner covers can be made in a variety of ways with leftover fabric. The easiest solution, although not the most attractive, is to simply cut 12-inch squares, baste the edges, and affix Velcro® tabs to the underside; matching tabs can be placed on the outside of the finished. If you have enough fabric on hand, you can make

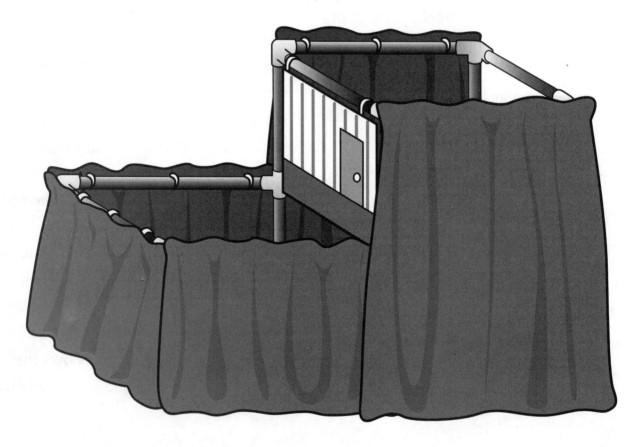

longer corner panels that cover the entire length of the corner.

When you travel, pack the stage by tying the long rods together with bungee cords, and the smaller ones in a large duffel bag.

Hang the curtains on trouser hangers to keep them fresh and wrinkle free.

With the help of a friend, you can make this project in a weekend. And this stage will serve you well in many venues!

chapter **eight** # Make a Scene

Imagination casts sunlight on the landscape of the mind. —Lois Keffer

SCENEBOARDS LITERALLY SET THE STAGE for your puppet productions. Building plywood sceneboards is a task for those who truly enjoy carpentry work, but it's not as hard as it may seem, even for carpenter wannabes and handyma'ams. And decorating them is especially fun. Enlist the help of artistic friends. After all, who doesn't like to make a scene now and then!

PROPBOARD

Before getting into the details (and fun) of constructing your sceneboards, you need to make a "propboard" for your stage. A propboard hangs parallel to and just behind the front bar of the stage. Make it from a 6-ft. long, lightweight wood strip, such as a "1 x 4". Cut the wood just slightly shorter than the width of the stage, then screw in a large hook at each end so the propboard will hang from the sidebars.

Add a strip of smooth, heavy-duty Velcro® that runs the entire length of the board, facing the puppeteers. The Velcro® must be strong enough to hold black lights and other props that you may need. Save the "sticky" Velcro® strips for these accessories.

Use Velcro®ed pinching clothespins to hold your scripts or agendas to the propboard.

Sceneboards

Sceneboards are backdrops that you can change for an endless number of puppet skit settings. Sceneboards enhance imagination and adds spectacle! And, in most cases, they're fun to make!

Cardboard vs. Foamcore

Sceneboards may be made from a variety of materials. While cardboard may be available in sheets as large as 6' x 4', cardboard tends to warp badly—especially when it's painted! You'll be sorely disappointed if you go this route. We even tried bracing cardboard with furring strips, but the boards warped, drew in, and generally got all lumpy and squeehawed and had to be thrown away.

Probably the most portable material is foamcore, but it's difficult to find in sheets longer than 3 or 4 feet long. Foamcore is readily available at most office supply stores—even Wal-Mart. One solution to not finding huge sheets is to duct-tape two or three sheets together to get a 6' x 4' backdrop. If you take advantage of this option, be sure you tape the seams of only one side—so it can fold for portability.

If you make your sceneboards from foamcore, keep a couple of things in mind: 1) You will have a seam on your backdrop (which really isn't a big deal, but it will lack the total realism of the wooden variety); 2) Foamcore dents very, very easily and can snap and break if not handled with extreme care. If you plan to transport your sceneboards frequently, keep the fragility of foamcore in mind. You might just opt for heavier plywood sceneboards for durability.

Plywood Sceneboards

Building plywood sceneboards is not for the faint of heart! But I can attest to the fact that anyone who is determined can make them. In fact, I "cut my carpentry teeth" on building them, and have since become a handyma'am of sorts!

Keep in mind that plywood backdrops require two able-bodied individuals to lift and hang on the puppet stage. If you have teen helpers around, you'll have no problem!

Materials

You will need the following for each sceneboard you construct:

- One sheet of lightweight (1/4 in. thick) plywood or Luan, 4' x 8'
- Furring strips (1" x 2" thick) in the following lengths:
  - 6.5 ft. (2 pieces)
  - 3.5 ft. (2 pieces)
  - 4 ft. (4 pieces)
- Wood glue
- 3/4-in. wood screws
- 4 screw hooks (1/2 in. screw end)
- Tools
- Drill with Phillips head drill bits (a hand screwdriver will work, but is time-consuming)
- Power saw
- Jigsaw (optional, for window cutting)
- Straight-edge yardstick or T-square
- Tape measure
- Pencil

Optional Supplies (for moveable doors)
- 2 Small hinges (for miniature doors)
- Wooden knob, (2" diameter)
- Extra furring strips

DIRECTIONS

Measuring and Cutting

Lay the plywood on the floor or on a very large worktable. From the edge, measure and mark a rectangle 6.5 ft. long and 3.5 ft. wide. Mark it with a straight edge and pencil. Then, using the power saw, cut carefully on the line. Save the scraps—they will be used for corner braces and other details.

Using a 6 ft. edge as the bottom, measure and cut out rectangles from the bottom corners, 6 in. high and 3.5 in. wide.

Optional Doors and Windows

If you want to add a door or window to your sceneboard, do all the cutting before it's framed up. By cutting first, you'll avoid having braces run right across the window or door opening! Draw doors from the

bottom of the panel. Make them 15 in. wide and 2.5. ft. tall. If it seems disproportionately tall, keep in mind that nobody will see the bottom six inches. This is where the puppeteer will hold and manipulate the door while the puppets "open" it and walk in and out! It's a great effect!

Your personal "room design" may require a center door, but I've found it best to place the door somewhere to the left or right of the center. It allows room for more furniture, trees (if it's outside the house), a window, and better bracing of the entire sceneboard. Think your designs through, front and back, before cutting! Avoid cutting doors and windows closer than one foot from the top so you don't compromise the strength of the sceneboard.

After you've cut the door, lay it back in place so you can position the hinges. Making sure the entire sheet of wood is front side up, place the hinge on the "wall," about two inches below the top of the door. Place the other hinge on the wall about eight inches from the bottom of the door (remember, the bottom six inches will not be visible). Using a power drill, drive the screws neatly through the holes, plywood, and into the furring strip behind it. Then, attach the door to the hinge. If the screws are too long and poke through the other side of the door, attach a little wood block (from leftover furring strips) to "catch" the screw as it comes through.

Disregarding the lower 6-inches of the door, position the knob at a place where it looks realistic—not too high on the door; slightly below center, and about 3 inches from the edge is best. Drill a small hole for the screw, and insert the screw from the back of the door and into the knob on the front. Now isn't that cute?

For windows, cut a 12-inch square. You can glue "panes" (a "plus" made of cardboard or wood) to the back.

Framing

Prepare your 6.5 ft. and 3.5 ft. furring strips in this way: Lay them flat, wide side down. Measure 2 inches from each end and draw a straight line across. Now draw a line from corner to corner and cut carefully on that diagonal line. Make SURE the diagonal cuts on each end are OPPOSITE each other.

Place the sceneboard face down on the floor or table, and line up the furring strips around the edges to form a frame. If you have a hole cut for a door, measure and cut a piece out of the bottom furring strip to allow for the open doorway. If the frame pieces do not require any further cutting for adjustment, glue them in place with wood glue and let them dry. If you don't have time to let them dry, just flip it all over, positioning the furring strips to the underneath edges by "feel", and drive wood screws into the sceneboard, 1 inch from the top, and into the furring strip. Do this all the way around the panel, keeping screws about 8 inches apart.

Bracing

Now flip the whole assembly over. Then take the 4 ft. pieces and lay them across the back of the frame about 2 ft. from the ends. Screw them into the frame securely to keep the frame from twisting in transport.

You may have to position the braces a bit to the left or to the right to avoid a window or door. You may even have to get real creative and brace diagonally. Do whatever it takes to strengthen the piece without adding too much bulk and weight.

Now for the corner braces. You can use your leftover plywood (*Don't mistakenly use your door if you've cut one out—it's happened before!*) Measure and cut two 10-inch squares. Then cut them diagonally so that you're left with four triangles. Place these triangles at the corners of your sceneboard and screw them into the frame. Wherever you can, screw them into the diagonal brace as well. This will really add strength to your sceneboard. Flip it all over and drive screws into your diagonal brace from the front (do this by "feel"—you can tap with a hammer to locate it).

For doors and windows, you may not actually need corner braces at all. If you want to strengthen them, cut two 2-inch squares of plywood, fit them in the corners and screw them in place. Then flip the sceneboard over and drive screws into all parts of the door frame that have not yet been secured. Do the same for the central cross brace.

Hanging

Screw hooks into the corners on the back of the sceneboards. Lift the sceneboard and set it so that the cutout corners rest on the side PVC pipes. Rest the back against the high pipes. Run a bungee cord through the

hook on the back of the sceneboard. Wrap it snugly around the nearby pipe, and run the other bungee hook back into the sceneboard hook. Do the same for the other three corners.

Decorating

Decorating the puppet sceneboards is a lot of fun. Be as creative as you like within these simple guidelines.

Be consistent in decorating to scale. Create everything in miniature to maintain the fantasy.

Avoid prepasted wallpaper unless you use extra adhesive. Prepasted wallpaper tends to bubble and pop off when the frames twist even the slightest bit. If you use wallpaper, be sure you glue it on by painting a strong adhesive evenly over the board before affixing the wallpaper. Contact paper actually works very well as wallpaper, although some bubbles may appear with twisting and warping of the frame. Contact paper and vinyl wallpaper offer the advantage of being sponge-wipeable.

Use a very tiny-print in your wallpaper. Contact paper comes in several miniature floral stripe prints which look very realistic in puppet houses—especially the puppet kitchen.

Use Velcro® and hot-glue when you accessorize. Hot glue is great for very small details, but Velcro® is really more reliable for larger objects. Use Velcro® tabs to hang little framed pictures on the wall and to secure items to shelves (things can get knocked off if you bump the stage).

Use matte paint. Glossy paint creates an annoying glare on the set, especially when you use a spotlight.

Creating Worlds in Miniature

Now we'll walk room by room through some wonderfully imaginative sets. You've done all the "grunt work." Here's where the fun begins!

The Kitchen

Put an entry door on one side and a refrigerator on the other. You can build a refrigerator that opens by framing a door (framing gives a 3-D effect) and attaching it with hinges. You can even paint or glue "groceries" inside. Make a refrigerator handle with a craft stick and two small pegs about 1 inch long or less. Hot-glue the pegs 1/2 inch from each end of the stick. Then glue the pegs to the fridge. Paint it silver for a truly realistic look!

Mount a little shelf (screw it on to a wood strip behind the wall) and load it with miniature groceries from toy stores. Hang realistic-looking toy utensils and a clock on the wall. If you've cut a window, hang cafe curtains with bows. Make it a real kitchen!

The Living Room

Put an entry door on one side, and a sofa on the other.
The sofa can be painted on. Cover the "back" with lightweight fabric. Cover the arms with a

plump layer of polyester fiberfill, even around the edges, then cover with the lightweight fabric (use hot glue to secure the fabric on the backside). Glue the 3 pieces to the sceneboard in their original positions, remembering that the bottom 6 inches will not be visible. The audience should see just below the wings of the arms.

Paint or "wallpaper" the walls. Create a TV

from an appropriately sized shallow box glued to the wall. Hang framed pictures of your puppet family for a homey effect.

Bedrooms

Bedrooms are easy! You can paint a headboard right onto the sceneboard or on foamcore. You may want a footboard to hang inside the prop bar. The footboard can have the "sticky" matching Velcro® tabs clued on it's "good side". Now you have a bed with a headboard and footboard, and your puppet can "sit" or "lie" on the bed. (Make sure you position your bed low enough to hide your arms when you operate the puppet.)

Screw a coat hook on the bedroom wall and

hang a little jacket or sweater or miniature bookbag. Hang posters—anything relevant to your character. It's *his* room!

Workshop

Glue a large piece of pegboard to the sceneboard and hang realistic-looking toy tools such as hammers, saws, screwdrivers and

wrenches—even little power tools!

House Exterior

Before cutting and framing your board, decide which side the house will be on and cut out the door and window. Your house should be about 3.5 ft. wide. Measure in from either end of the board and draw a line at that point from top to bottom. Measure and cut our your door and window. Now you will need a roof. Use extra

plywood or sturdy cardboard or foamcore for this. The roof should be kind of a squatty triangle—short and wide—and the bottom should be positioned about 8 inches from the top of the sceneboard (more if it would otherwise be top heavy). The width should extend about 10 inches beyond the sides of the house. But it cannot be so high as to scrape your ceiling—worse yet, not even fit! Just make sure it covers the corners of the house when placed at least 8 inches down on the sceneboard. Include a little chimney, if you like, either cut out with the roof, or added on later in cardboard or foamcore.

After you frame the board, attach the roof to the outside of the house with screws, securing them into the wood frame behind the sceneboard.

A simple, but effective color scheme is to paint the area surrounding the house is clear sky blue; paint the house solid yellow; red door and window frame; black roof. Paint green shrubs around the house. If you'd like, create a window box in front of the window and fill it with silk flowers. Make panes from plywood or from an old yardstick —just make a cross to fit the window and glue it to the back of the window and paint it red to match the door. Hang a curtain behind the entire window. Your puppets can even peek out this window from time to time.

SIMPLEST OF ALL

While "convertible" sceneboards may not be as exciting in some ways, they may be more practical for some ministries. You can save money by creating a basic room with a door, paint it blue (blue is adaptable for all rooms and genders), and use Velcro® tabs to put up and take down accessories, such as pictures, pegboards, headboards, footboards, cardboard refrigerators, shelves, etc. Just make sure each room has an accessory to hang on each of the tabs.

More Shopping Fun!

Be on the look out for fun things to enhance your puppet stages. Here are some of them:

- Single-serving cereal boxes
- Miniature picture frames
- Small-print contact paper
- Small-print fabrics for curtains
- Toy household items—appliances, dishes, etc.
- Miniature books

Building and decorating sets can be a lot of fun. Start simple and work your way up as time and resources allow. Recruit some friends to help you, and have a ball!

chapter nine Sound, Lights and Special Effects

Kids are like squirrels— they're attracted to anything shiny. —K. L. Park

NOTHING GRABS AND HOLDS AN AUDIENCE like spectacle—unusual sights and sounds. And there are a whole host of great, fun-to-do special effects you can add to your puppet shows.

Before we get to the special things you can do, let's go over the basics of sound and light. After the work you put into your puppet productions, you definitely want to be seen and heard! Usually, ordinary room light is enough to pull off a great puppet show. But sound is another matter.

SOUND

If your puppeteers are doing the talking, they may need microphones, especially if one puppeteer is loud and the other has a very soft voice that doesn't carry well through the curtains. Headset mikes are best. Lapel mikes may pick up rustling noises from your clothing when you move. If you can't afford headset mikes (corded or cordless are available) you may have to resort to the boom-stand variety. It's a challenge to use boom stands without bumping them as you move the puppets around. Bumping into the stand creates thumping noises and feedback, which downgrade the sound of your production. If you don't have headset mikes, the best alternative is pre-recording.

GET IT ON TAPE

You'll find lots of advantages to pre-recording or using professionally produced programs. You can play the tapes back on a portable stereo or sound system while the puppets lip sync. Let's explore some of the benefits of pre-recording.

- Your puppeteers don't have to have "theatre voices"
- Everyone can concentrate on puppet movement
- When your puppeteers practice at home, they can hear and respond to the other puppets' parts while they learn their own lines
- Your puppet voices will always be heard equally
- No one will ever "drop" a line
- You will always know the length of time of your production for scheduling purposes
- There will never be any "surprises" in your materials
- Sound effects can be built right into the taped program rather than produced on the spot

- It's easier to find a last-minute substitute for an absent puppeteer if the material is on tape.

I hope I've convinced you to start off with taped programs. Even professional puppeteers appreciate the reliability of pre-recording.

SPECIAL SOUNDS

Great programs are available on tape from a variety of puppet ministries. If you choose to write and pre-record your own materials, you'll find that sound effects add a lot of zip and zing. Here are some ideas:

- Tape footsteps for entries and exits, being sure to fade them in and out..
- Record the sound of clinking dishes if your puppets are dining. The sound of a spoon in a china cup works well.
- Record beeper sounds or telephone rings.
- If your puppet is on the phone, you may want to record the voice on the other side of the line. To do this, use a phone with an extension in another room. Take two phones off the hook and wait a minute until the warning beep and off-hook messages are over. Now your actor

can speak into the phone in one room while you record his voice through the ear piece in the other.

☺ Appliances and tools add power to your program! Consider using blenders, hair dryers, drills, and saws.

☺ Birds, lions, other animals—your local library or major music store should have CDs with plenty of animal sounds.

☺ Thunder is available on CDs of sound effects. Check your music stores.

☺ Record cars going by on a busy street. Be sure to tape long enough to get good background for your entire show. Make sure your background noise isn't overpowering. Be subtle.

☺ It's fun to add mood music and punch-line noises. If you know of a good musician with a synthesizer, you may be able to arrange him or her to record some wacky noises or musical interludes during funny spots in your show. To get ideas for how to approach this, watch a cartoon this week and listen to the way music is used to emphasize humor. Mood music is also effective for sad or poignant moments.

You'll want to be careful not to overdo background music or noise. Like Tabasco sauce, it adds zings, but a little goes a long way!

LIGHT

While room light is probably enough for a basic show, you may want to use a spotlight for special occasions. Here are other ways to use lights for special dramatic effect.

Strobe Lights

Strobe lights (high-speed flashing lights) can be effective in certain scenes, such as dream scenes, depictions of destruction, wild party life, and others. Please bear in mind this important safety note: strobe lights have been known to trigger epileptic seizures when flash rates exceed 5 per second. While such occurrences are rare, it's best to set your strobe light at a safe level.

Black Light

Black light puppet productions present an entirely new and exciting aspect to the world of puppetry! But you must have a room that is totally dark—that means either no windows, or blackened windows (taped up with cardboard). Blinds alone won't do. It has to be pitch black. Black lights need to be mounted on the prop bar, on the left and right.

Black light is invisible, ultraviolet light that reflects certain materials—especially certain fluorescent colors and most things that are white. Dark colors, certain greens, browns, navy blue and dark reds are invisible—or nearly invisible— under black light. This phenomenon creates a wonderful setting for certain kinds of puppet productions.

Not all puppets will show up under black light, so you'll need to "audition" your puppets under the light well in advance. Just because a puppet is light colored—even white—does not mean it will show up under black light. If you really have your heart set on black light programming, you may need to make or purchase puppets for that express purpose.

Black light performances are best used as short segments, such as a song, with several characters taking turns appearing. This keeps the audience "wowed" by the entrances of curiously glowing critters.

I've seen black-light puppets that were nothing more than giant mouths with lips, teeth and tongue—great for "singing" when surrounded by black-light guitars, saxophones and other instruments. For accessories to your show, you can make simple foamcore instruments using enlarged clip art, and coloring them with fluorescent paint or markers. Mount them on black sticks and bounce them around while a puppet sings.

In your programs, a group of white-gloved human hands can be choreographed in very interesting ways. Be sure the owners of the hands wear black, long sleeved shirts, so only the hands will show under the black light. It's lots of fun to see white hands floating and maneuvering together in choreographed "dance."

Let your imagination run when you plan black light shows. You can do awesome space themes, underwater themes, jungle themes and Vaudeville Show themes with Christian scripts. Just be sure to check your puppets in advance to make sure they shine in the black light.

Light Stands

Professional light stands used by photographers are very effective in lighting the puppet stage from both sides. They are lightweight and portable, and can illuminate the stage, eliminating the need for house lights. Having the house lights down always decreases distractions in the audience and lends a special showtime feeling.

If you choose not to purchase light stands, use house lights during your shows instead of trying to light only from underneath (from the prop bar) unless you're using black light. White light from the floor (or prop bar) only illuminates the puppets' chins and has an eerie effect, which isn't usually what you're after.

Colored Lights

Colored lights can add wonderful effects. Blue light makes great night scenes. Red sometimes indicates trouble or violence. Green is effective in dark forest scenes. You can use colored bulbs, or purchase lighting "gels"—colored transparent sheets that you affix over the "can" of a stage light fixture (regular cellophane wrap is not brilliant enough). Gels can be purchased at a professional lighting equipment store.

Some large sound equipment retailers may carry it as well.

Fog Machines

Nothing creates an ethereal mood like a light blanket of fog hanging low in the air. Linseed-oil smoke machines can be purchase or rented from theatre supply houses. Be warned that fog machines can be difficult to control. You need lots of practice to maintain a light fog—especially in a small puppet set. You don't want huge cumulus clouds of smoke unless your script calls for it. And a heavy layer of linseed oil smoke can be hard on your puppeteers.

Dry Ice

For puppet programs, you may only need dry ice and water to produce the fog you desire. You can get dry ice from some pharmaceutical companies, meat packing companies and other places where cold transport is common. A large block of dry ice in a dishpan of water will bubble and emit a lazy white cloud. You may want to build cardboard flanges around your pan to concentrate the cloud and give it direction. Just experiment with it until you get the desired effect. Place the pan on a stool to raise it high enough to be seen. Dry ice is a less expensive, easier-to-control alternative to a smoke machine.

SCRIM AND BACKLIGHT

One of the most effective ways to produce "dreams" or angelic "visitations" is with the use of a cheesecloth scrim and back lighting. Using a scrim as your backdrop curtain, your backdrop can be opaque when lit from the front. But when it's lit from behind, the audience can suddenly see through the wall and into another dimension!

To create this effect, you need to choose the right kind of theatre muslin—a thin cheesecloth. Be careful not to choose cheesecloth that's too thin, or you'll be able to see through it before the back light surprise.

Remove your backdrop curtain and stretch the cheesecloth tightly over the backdrop area. Secure it with Velcro. If you need a scene on the cheesecloth, use fabric dye rather than paint. Paint will clog the pores of the weave and make the cheesecloth opaque. Use a very light touch with the dye. Work near the edges first to see how much the dye bleeds.

When you use this "dream cloth", the houselights and frontlights should be down. The walls of the back section of the puppet stage should be completely covered with curtains or sheets. The lighting inside the back section can be accomplished in several ways—choose the way you can afford and experiment with the lights you have available. Ideally, you could have lights mounted inside, on the side pipes, below "stage floor" level. These lights should be connected to a single switch so they come on at the same time. While the dream is going on, your puppet in pajamas can "watch" from the front stage section. It's a very effective spectacle.

MILKSHAKES AND PIES IN THE FACE

The secret of Jasper's milkshake splattering out of the open blender is:

spray foam rug cleaner!

Rug cleaner is used to clean puppets, so it won't harm your puppet. You can even fill a little pot-pie tin with the foam and throw it in the face of your puppet for a clown show.

One important thing to remember is that some rug cleaners irritate the nose and lungs if you get caught in the spray. I used a new rug cleaner one night when I performed Jasper's milkshake routine, and nearly choked in the tent! The spray gave

off a peppery odor and I could not breathe until the spray settled. Fortunately, I could hold my breath that long. Needless to say, I went back to my old brand!

Also, use caution when spraying any chemical around hot lights. Some chemicals are combustible. It's always a good idea to keep a fire extinguisher handy when you're using powerful lighting.

HAVE FUN experimenting with these special effects. They're the cherry on top of your sundae!

Puppet Show Today

When love and skill work together
expect a masterpiece. —John Ruskin

SOCK PUPPETS

Sock puppets are among the most common
because they're easy to make and because
everybody—at least everybody I know—
owns a pair of socks!

Sock Puppet

This is the old fashioned mitten variety,
with a moving mouth. It's
You'll need:

- ☺ a clean (!) tube sock
- ☺ corrugated cardboard scraps
- ☺ polyester fiberfill, cotton, or
  another old sock
- ☺ scissors
- ☺ fabric glue
- ☺ tracing paper and pencil

- ☺ Optional: wiggly eyes, buttons, felt,
  yarn, and anything else you want to
  decorate with

Trace the mouthpiece onto tracing paper
and cut it out. Then lay it on a piece of
cardboard and trace two pieces. Cut them
out. Turn the sock inside out and smooth it.
Apply fabric glue to one of the
cardboard pieces. Align the straight
edge of the cardboard with the
edge of the toe seam and press it
firmly. Turn the sock over
and apply the other
piece of cardboard in the same way.

Let the pieces dry completely

before turning the sock to the right side. Once you do, push the center seam into the sock so the mouth is formed. Stuff a bit of fiberfill into the top of the head. Cut out an oval of red felt to fit the inside of the mouth. Glue it with the fabric glue. Add wiggly eyes, or eyes made of felt. Top with yarn hair or a tuft of craft fur! There you have it! A sock puppet!

Glove Puppet (moving arms)

You can always take a glove, stick a ping pong ball head on the index finger and make a puppet. Or you can make a glove puppet with a little help from your sewing machine. Here's a cute (and too easy!) bunny glove puppet pattern that can be adapted for a variety of animals:

You'll need:

- two 12" squares of craft fur
- buttons
- felt scraps
- glove puppet pattern [ART: include in patterns],
- tracing paper and pencil
- scissors
- fabric glue
- needle and thread
- two little white pompons, and a little pink one (or felt will do)

Trace the pattern to the tracing paper. Cut it out, then pin it to two layers of craft fur, placed fur side together. Cut them out. Before separating the pieces, stitch the edges together all around, leaving only the bottom open.

Turn the puppet to the right side. Cut out two bunny ears. Position them where you want them on the puppet, then stitch them

in place by hand from the inside.

Next, stitch on button eyes or glue on scraps of felt. You can use two white pompons for a muzzle, with a tiny pink pompon for the nose. It's done!

Use the same furry foundation to make bears, cats, dogs, and mice. Only the ears need to change!

Rubber-Band-Mouth Puppets
Grubber Band Clan

Kids will learn how fun resourcefulness can be when they put these great puppets together from tool room junk!

You'll need:
- ☺ Old paintbrushes, putty spreaders or feather dusters
- ☺ Small rubber bands (thicker is better)
- ☺ Odds and ends from your toolbox—be creative and resourceful!
- ☺ E-6000 adhesive (hot glue will not work on metal surfaces)
- ☺ Strand of thread

1. Help each kid select an old tool for the head of a "grublet" puppet—a big old paintbrush, wide putty knife, even a whisk broom will work. Grubby stains and splatters will just add individuality to your grublet!

2. Search through your tool box, basement or junk drawers for objects to use for the eyes and nose. Some examples include nuts, washers, rubber rings, etc. If possible, ask kids to bring some items from their junk drawers at home. Set out all the items where kids can choose freely.

3. Show kids how to place the rubber band where the mouth should be. Lay it so that the flattest, or least curved, part of the rubber band forms the upper lip (i.e., so that the curves form the corners of the mouth).

4. Glue only the upper lip of the mouth to the grublet's face. Glue all other facial parts evenly.

5. After the glue has dried thoroughly, tie a long thread to the center of the lower lip (rubber band). Run it through the handle hole, if there is one (this just hides the thread a bit more). When you pull the thread, the mouth will open! Give it slack, and the mouth will pop closed again!

If you just can't stop there...

Nail carpet tacks to the sides of the wooden handles near the "head." Tie rubber-tube arms to the tacks with fishing line. Glue on hands made of whatever tool room junk you can find! Attach thin dowels to the "hands" to move the arms. Add aluminum foil clothing, if desired.

Box Puppets

You've heard of bag puppets. But how 'bout a box puppet? These are lots more fun and just about as easy to make!

You'll need:

- Large size gelatin box for each child
- Construction paper
- Glue
- Scissors
- Markers

1. Have kids tape the top panels of the boxes closed. Cut the boxes evenly across the front and side panels and crease the back panel so the box halves fold together, back-to-back. What were once the top and bottom panels are now parts of the face of the puppet!

2. Help kids measure the face and draw an oval or circle of construction paper that's slightly larger all around. Cut that piece in half. This forms the top of the face and the lower jaw. Once kids get the hang of it, they can make puppets with faces with higher foreheads and shorter chins.

3. Show kids how to put the parts of the face together on a flat surface and color in lips along the edge where the halves meet. Draw eyes and a nose, and make hair from strips of construction paper. If

you'd like, you can curl the hair by either coiling the strips by hand or by running the strip over a scissor edge the way you curl ribbon.

4. Glue the face halves to the two panels of the box that form the face area. Cover the rest of the box with construction paper.

5. Make your puppet talk!

Try using yarn for hair. Make a whole family with different sized boxes!

FINGER PUPPETS

Finger puppets are nothing more than your own fingers—with a little embellishment. You'll need:

- old, tight-fitting gloves
- scissors
- washable, fine-tipped markers
- fabric glue and felt scraps

Use a washable marker to make small dot-eyes on your fingers, halfway between the last finger joint and the tip. For a sweater, cut the finger off of a knit glove. Then cut off the top 1-inch. Slip the longer piece over your finger, leaving the top joint uncovered. Then slip the top 1-inch piece onto your finger tip without covering the eyes. Roll the edges up to form a knit cap. That's it!

The thumb of the glove can make a great dog puppet. Glue little felt teardrops to the sides for ears. Use teeny felt scraps for eyes. Now, take a bow (wow)!

You can create lots of characters using yarn hair and white glue (it's washable) and fabric scraps. Use your imagination!

EASY MARIONETTES

Matchbox Marionette

This little matchbox guy is really "on fire for God!" Just watch him dance when you pull the strings!

You'll need:

- Small, empty matchbox (not a matchbook) for each child
- Two drinking straws for each child
- String
- Chenille wire
- large marshmallow
- Hole punch

1. Remove the matchbox "drawer." Careful placement of holes is important. If kids are punching their own holes, you'll want to supervise carefully. Punch a hole

in each flinted (striking) side near one end. Punch matching holes in the drawer. Punch leg holes in the bottom side of the drawer. Replace the drawer.

2. Cut the straws into six 2-inch pieces. Run a string through two pieces of the straw, then into one of the leg holes in the drawer and out the other.

3. Continue threading the string through two more pieces of straw. Tie 2-inch pieces of chenille wire to each end of the string and coil them for "feet." Run another string through one piece of straw, into an armhole in the matchbox, through the torso and out the other armhole. Continue running the string through another straw piece. Tie the ends to one-inch pieces of chenille wire and coil the wires into round "hands."

4. Use a pin or needle to poke a tiny neck hole. Push a 2-inch piece of chenille wire

halfway through the hole so it fits tightly.

5. Use a needle to run a string through the marshmallow. Tie the string to the bottom of the chenille "neck" and slip the marshmallow over wire snugly.

6. Tie strings to the string at the knee joints of both legs. Draw all three strings (two knee, one head) up evenly, making sure the puppet's legs are straight.

7. Make a cross out of plastic straws secured with chenille wire.

8. Tie one leg string to each side of the cross piece and the head string to the long stem of the cross. Tilt the cross side to side and the puppet will dance!

For a bigger puppet…
Make a big marionette using a cereal box body, mac-and-cheese-box head, and paper-towel-roll limbs! Use yarn instead of string, and make the cross out of paint-stirrers!

BASIC ANIMAL PUPPETS
MONKEY

Materials:
- 1/3 yard dark brown or grisled craft fur
- 6-inch square of white fur
- Scraps of tan, pink, and maroon or dark red felt
- Two 24mm craft animal eyes *(we recommend orange with large black pupils)*
- Scraps of cardboard
- Fabric glue
- Needle and thread or optional sewing machine

Procedure: Using a photocopier, enlarge the pattern on page R•51 200% so that the squares on the grid measure 1". Assemble as follows:

BODY

1.) With right sides together, cut two pieces of brown fur using pattern "B." The direction of the fur should be lengthwise on both pieces.
2.) Pin the two pieces of "B" with right sides together. Stitch together, 1/4" from the edge, following from point "AA" to point "BB," then to point "CC."
3.) Lay pattern "A" on a single layer of dark fur and cut out 1 piece. Fur direction should also be lengthwise. Cut slit as indicated.
4.) Lay fur pieces "A" and "B" together, right sides together. Pin all the way around the edge from "DD"" to "EE," then stitch.
5.) Turn stitched body inside-out and set aside.

MOUTH MITTEN

1.) Cut upper mouth pieces from tan felt, using patter piece "I." Be sure that one piece has a 1/4" tab at the bottom.
2.) Lay pieces on top of each other. *(If fabric other than felt is used, place right sides together.)* Stitch from "AA" to "BB" using a 1/4" seam. Turn inside out.
3.) Cut cardboard for mouth using pattern "J" and trim to fit inside the upper mouth pocket. Repeat process for lower mouth piece using pattern "G." Use tan felt *(without tab)* for the tongue. Use pattern "H" for the cardboard.
4.) Center finished mouth pieces with the tabs together. Stitch tabs together at base of mouth pieces to create a hinge. *(See Fig. 1)*

FACE

1.) Cut 1 each of "C" and "D" from white fur. Also cut 1 piece of "C" from white felt. Place felt piece "C" against the mouth mitten so that straight edges of "C" and the top layer of the mouth are aligned. Stitch together, leaving a 1/3" edge.
2.) Take the entire mitten and place it within the facial slit so the mitten opens on the inside of the puppet, and the muzzle and white felt are outside.
3.) Stitch the outer edges of the mitten around the facial slit from the inside. You may need to stitch this by hand. Then carefully hand stitch or glue *(with fabric glue)* the white fur face in place on the front of the puppet *(on top of the white felt)*. Trim the fur to fit if necessary. Place "D" beard snugly under the muzzle and stitch or glue securely.
4.) After the mouth and face are assembled, glue cardboard into mouth mitten by gluing TOP of lower cardboard *("H")* and BOTTOM of upper cardboard *("I")*. IMPORTANT: It is essential to get this right for the puppet to work properly.

EYES and NOSE

1.) Cut eye rims from pink felt using pattern "F" and lay them in place on the white fur. Poke holes through felt and fur for eye stems. Put eyes in place over the rims and secure inside puppet with stem caps.
2.) Cut nose from pink felt scrap using pattern "K" and glue on top of muzzle.

EARS

1.) Using pattern "E," cut 2 dark fur ears, and 2 pink felt pieces. Glue the pink pieces to the wrong side of the fur pieces.
2.) Bend the corners in so that they overlap in the center *(see Fig. 2)*. Stitch in place. Place ears on head *(10 o'clock and 2 o'clock positions)* and hand stitch from the inside.

FINISHING

1.) Trim bottom as needed. Hem may not be necessary, depending on fur used.

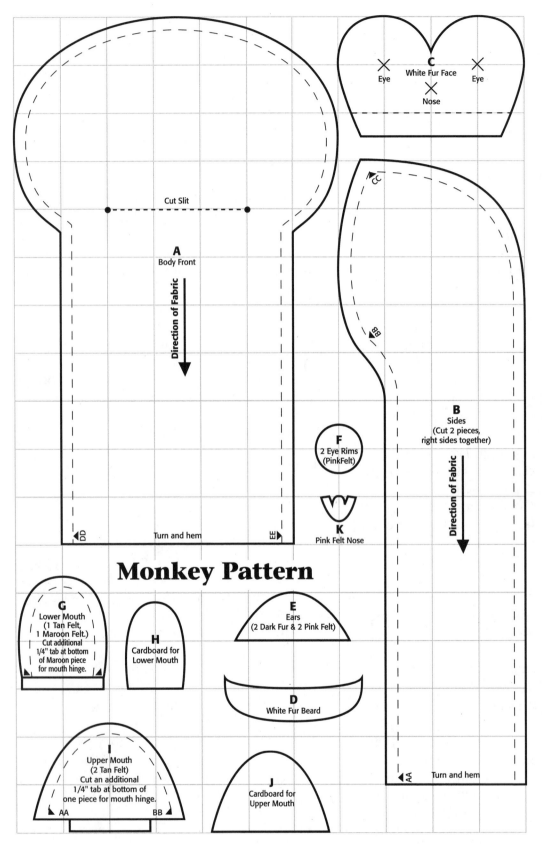

Monkey Pattern

A
Body Front

Cut Slit

Direction of Fabric

Turn and hem

DD   EE

C
White Fur Face
× Eye   × Eye
× Nose

B
Sides
(Cut 2 pieces,
right sides together)

Direction of Fabric

CC

BB

AA   Turn and hem

F
2 Eye Rims
(Pink Felt)

K
Pink Felt Nose

G
Lower Mouth
(1 Tan Felt,
1 Maroon Felt.)
Cut additional
1/4" tab at bottom
of Maroon piece
for mouth hinge.

H
Cardboard for
Lower Mouth

E
Ears
(2 Dark Fur & 2 Pink Felt)

D
White Fur Beard

I
Upper Mouth
(2 Tan Felt)
Cut an additional
1/4" tab at bottom of
one piece for mouth hinge.

AA   BB

J
Cardboard for
Upper Mouth

Scale: 1 square = 1"

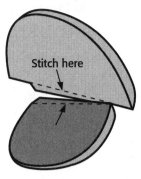

**Fig. 1
Mouth Assembly**

1.) Center upper mouth piece over lower mouth piece, tabbed sides together.

2.) Stitch bottom edge of upper mouth piece to top edge of lower mouth piece at the tabs, creating a hinge where the two pieces meet.

NOTE: Approximately 1/2" of upper mouth piece will extend beyond lower mouth piece on both sides.

Stitch here

Felt
Fur   Fur

**Fig. 2
Ear Assembly**

1.) Glue felt ear piece to inside of fur ear piece.

2.) Bring two ends of ear piece toward bottom center of ear, fur side out.

3.) Stitch in place.

FROG

Materials:

- 1/3 yard black and white patterned knit fabric
- 1/4 yard red or orange knit fabric *(such as velour)*
- White felt scraps
- Black felt scraps
- Two 18mm black animal eyes with fasteners
- All-purpose craft glue
- Polyester stuffing
- White thread
- Poster board or thin cardboard

* Note: use 1/4" seam allowances throughout.

HEAD & BODY

1.) Cut the following from the red or orange knit fabric: 1 of "A1" the head; 1 of "B1" the throat; 2 of "D1" sides of head. Add 1/2" of fabric at the bottom of each piece for the seam allowance.

2.) Cut the following from the black and white knit fabric: 1 each of "A2" the back *(add 6 1/2" of fabric to the bottom of the pattern piece)*; 1 each of "B2" the front *(add 3" of fabric to the bottom of the pattern piece)*; and 2 each of "D2" the sides *(add 2" of fabric to the bottom of the pattern piece.)*

3.) Sew the head and throat pieces to the body pieces using 1/4" seams. Sew "A1" to "A2;" sew "B1" to "B2;" sew both pieces of "D1" to "D2."

4.) Cut 2 eye rims, "E" from white felt. Cut a small slash in the center of each eye. Make a small slash at each eye placement of the sides of the head. Insert the eyes through the rims and the right sides of the head at the eye placement. Fasten from the wrong side of the fabric.

5.) Pin "A1" and "A2," the head and back, to the sides, "D1" and "D2," matching notches AA and BB. Sew using 1/4" seams.

MOUTH

1.) Cut 2 pieces of "C" out of black felt. Cut one of the pieces in half following the cutting line on the pattern piece. Lay the cut pieces on the uncut circle. Stitch close to the edge around the entire circle to create the mouth mitten.

2.) Pin "C" to the head matching the notches "EE-top." The right side of the head fabric should lay against the uncut circle. Sew the entire half circle using a 1/4" seam.

3.) Pin the other half of "C" to the throat and front "B1 and B2, " matching the notches "EE-bottom." The right side of the throat fabric should lay against the uncut circle. Pin the remaining side seams also. Beginning at the bottom of the puppet, sew the side seams and remaining half of the mouth mitten.

4.) Cut the cardboard for the mouth. Trim to fit inside the mitten if necessary. Put a thin layer of glue on one side of a piece of cardboard. Insert the cardboard into the upper part of the mouth mitten with the glue on the bottom side. Put glue on one side of the other piece of cardboard. Insert the cardboard into the lower part of the mouth mitten with the glue on the top side.

5.) Carefully turn the puppet right side out.

FINISHING

1.) Stuff the puppet's head with polyester stuffing.

2.) Optional: If desired, cut a small piece of fabric. Hand-stitch this fabric over the polyester stuffing on the inside of the puppet. This will keep the stuffing from moving while the puppet is in use.

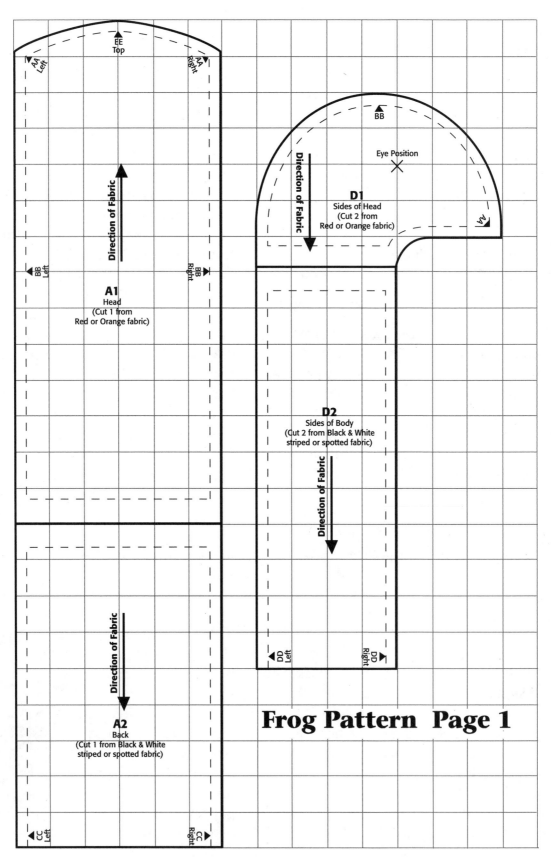

Frog Pattern Page 1

Scale: 1 square = 3/4"

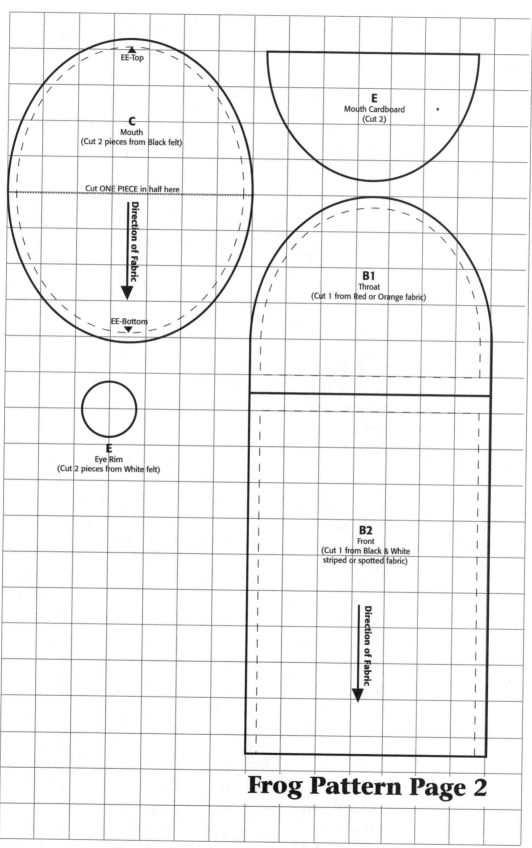

C
Mouth
(Cut 2 pieces from Black felt)

EE-Top

Cut ONE PIECE in half here

Direction of Fabric

EE-Bottom

E
Mouth Cardboard
(Cut 2)

E
Eye Rim
(Cut 2 pieces from White felt)

B1
Throat
(Cut 1 from Red or Orange fabric)

B2
Front
(Cut 1 from Black & White
striped or spotted fabric)

Direction of Fabric

Frog Pattern Page 2

Scale: 1 square = 3/4"

BIRD

Materials:

- 1/4 yard gray felt or napped felt
- Red maribou feather boa, approximately 4 ft. long
- Red chenille wires
- Scraps of white, pink, and black felt
- 1 square of yellow felt
- Two 18-mm. animal craft eyes with fasteners
- All-purpose craft glue
- Floral tape
- Thread: red and gray
- Polyester stuffing

* Note: Use 1/4-inch seams unless indicated.

FEATHER CREST

1.) Cut the boa into eight pieces, 10" long. Cut a chenille wire for each piece of boa.

2.) Using a doubled strand of thread, tie each boa securely to a wire in at least three places from bottom to top. Leave 1" of the boa on top of the wire.

3.) Cut eight 1/2" circles of black felt. Glue one circle to the top of each boa. Hold the finished boa and wire pieces together like a bouquet. Wrap the wire ends tightly together with floral tape. Cover any sharp ends of the wire.

BODY

1.) Cut two pieces of the head and body "A" from the gray felt. Mark the mouth slit and eye markings on one piece of fabric on the wrong side.

2.) Cut the mouth slit. A rotary cutter can be used for this.

3.) Cut two eye rims, "C," from white felt. Punch holes in the center of each rim. Cut a small slit at each eye marking. Poke an animal eye through an eye rim and the right side of the face. Fasten on the wrong side of the fabric. Repeat for the other eye.

4.) With the right sides together, stitch both pieces of "A" together stitching from AA to BB and CC to DD.

BEAK

1.) Cut two pieces of yellow felt using pattern piece "B," the beak. Cut one piece in half following the cutting line on "B." Lay the cut pieces on the uncut piece. Stitch close to the edge all the way around the beak. Turn right side out. This is the beak mitten.

2.) From the wrong side of the head fabric, insert the beak mitten through the mouth slit. Hand stitch the beak mitten into place, keeping 1/8 inch of the felt on the inside of the puppet. Turn the puppet right side out.

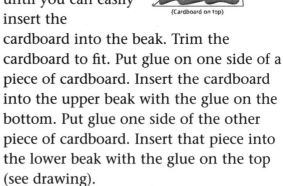

3.) Cut two pieces of cardboard using pattern piece "D." Turn the puppet inside out only until you can easily insert the cardboard into the beak. Trim the cardboard to fit. Put glue on one side of a piece of cardboard. Insert the cardboard into the upper beak with the glue on the bottom. Put glue one side of the other piece of cardboard. Insert that piece into the lower beak with the glue on the top (see drawing).

4.) Cut one inner mouth, "E," from pink felt. Glue inner mouth to the inside of the beak.

FINISHING

1.) Insert the "stem" of the feather crest between the two seams at the top of the head. Allow 2" to remain inside the puppet. Hand-stitch the crest securely in place.

2.) Stuff the top of the puppet with polyester stuffing. Pack the stuffing around the stem of the crest to keep it from moving.

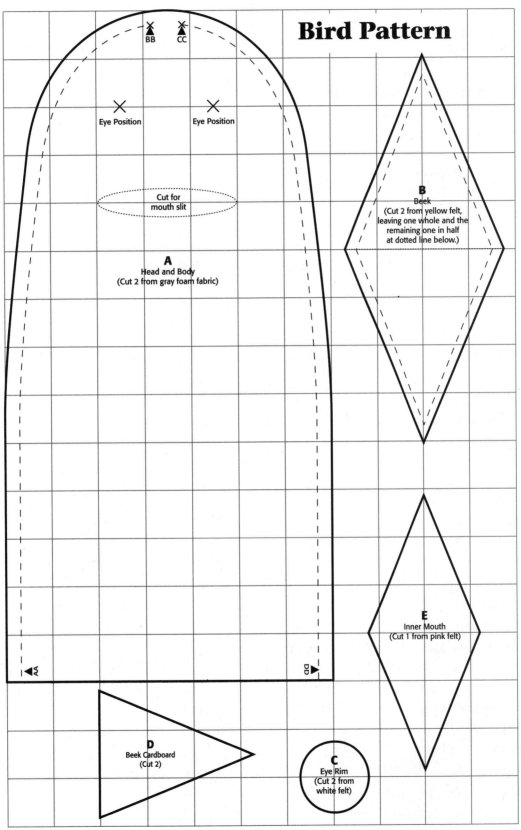

Bird Pattern

Eye Position   Eye Position

Cut for
mouth slit

A
Head and Body
(Cut 2 from gray foam fabric)

B
Beek
(Cut 2 from yellow felt,
leaving one whole and the
remaining one in half
at dotted line below.)

E
Inner Mouth
(Cut 1 from pink felt)

D
Beek Cardboard
(Cut 2)

C
Eye Rim
(Cut 2 from
white felt)

Scale: 1 square = 1"

JAGUAR

Materials:

- 1/2 yard jaguar or leopard fur
- Black felt
- Scraps of red and tan felt
- Craft animal eyes (15 – 20 mm in size)
- Craft whiskers (optional)
- Polyester stuffing
- Cardboard
- All-purpose craft glue
- Thread to match fur fabric

BODY and EARS

1.) Cut the following from fur fabric: 2 of "A" Sides of head; 1 of "D" Back of head; 1 of "C" Snout and Top of head; 1 of "E" Throat and Body front.

2.) With rights sides together, match points AA and BB of pieces "C" and "D." Pin together and sew from AA to BB using 1/4" seams.

3.) Cut 2 fur ears and 2 tan felt ears using pattern "J." Glue a tan felt ear to the wrong side of a fur ear. Repeat with the other ear. Match point JJ on the ears with point JJ on the sides of head "A." The felt should lay against the fur of "A." Pin ears so the flat ends will be in the seam.

4.) Take one of the "A" pieces and place it, right sides together, against "C/D," matching points CC on the snout and side of head. Match points DD on both pieces and pin them as well. Continue to pin the pieces together, turning piece "C" along the curve of "A" until the entire piece is pinned together. (The ear will be pinned into this seam.) Sew together using a 1/4" seam.

5.) Do the same for the other side, once again matching the pieces with right sides together. After pinning, sew together using a 1/4" seam.

6.) With rights sides together, match points EE and HH on "E" Throat and Body front with the sides of head piece "A." Stitch each seam using a 1/4" seam.

EYES and NOSE

1.) With the patterns provided, trace the eyes and nose on black felt and paint with white paint as indicated. If you prefer, you can use purchased craft animal eyes and nose instead of making your own. The felt eyes and nose can be glued in place after you complete the mouth. (If you are using purchased eyes and nose, wait until after the mouth is in place to position these.)

MOUTH

1.) With rights sides together, out of tan felt cut 1 of "H" Mouth.

2.) With right sides together, match points CC, FF, and GG on the mouth piece and the puppet. Sew around the entire mouth piece using 1/4" seams.

3.) Turn the puppet so that right side of the fabric is facing out.

4.) Cut 2 pieces of cardboard using pattern pieces "L1" and "L2." Insert (and glue) into the upper and lower mouth.

5.) Cut the tongue out of red felt using pattern piece "I." Hand stitch or glue the tongue it into the mouth area in the appropriate place.

6.) Stuff head with polyester stuffing.

7.) At this time, place the eyes and nose on the puppet if you have not already done so. Place the whiskers on the side of Jaguar's muzzle and hand stitch into place.

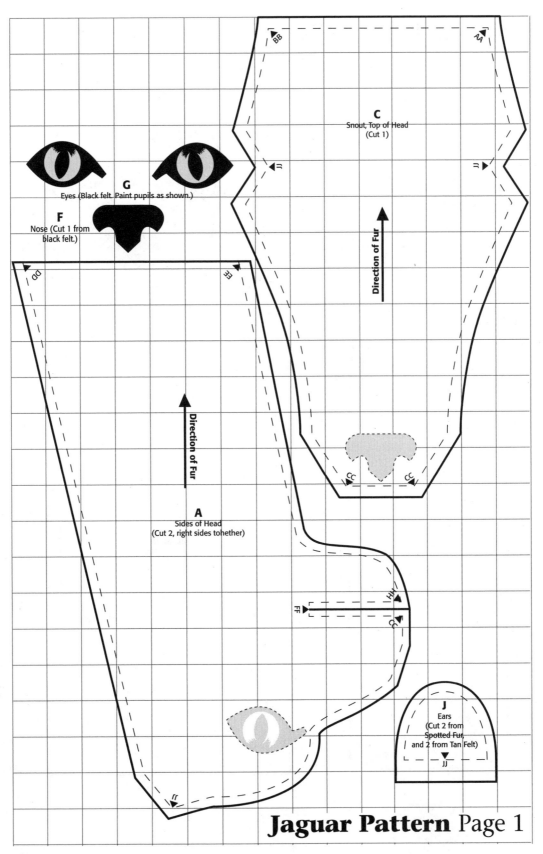

C
Snout, Top of Head
(Cut 1)

Direction of Fur

G
Eyes (Black felt. Paint pupils as shown.)

F
Nose (Cut 1 from black felt.)

Direction of Fur

A
Sides of Head
(Cut 2, right sides tohether)

J
Ears
(Cut 2 from Spotted Fur, and 2 from Tan Felt)

Jaguar Pattern Page 1

Scale: 1 square = 3/4"

Jaguar Pattern Page 2

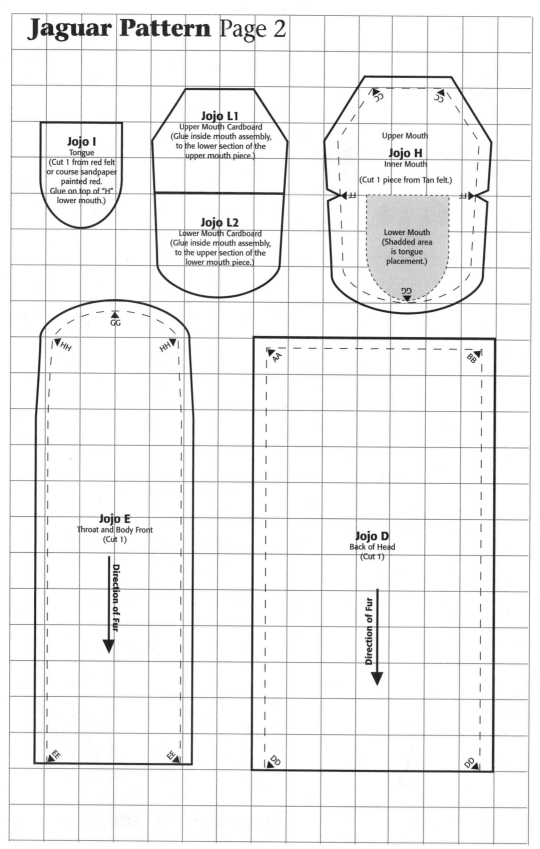

Jojo I
Tongue
(Cut 1 from red felt
or course sandpaper
painted red.
Glue on top of "H"
lower mouth.)

Jojo L1
Upper Mouth Cardboard
(Glue inside mouth assembly,
to the lower section of the
upper mouth piece.)

Jojo L2
Lower Mouth Cardboard
(Glue inside mouth assembly,
to the upper section of the
lower mouth piece.)

Upper Mouth
Jojo H
Inner Mouth

(Cut 1 piece from Tan felt.)

Lower Mouth
(Shadded area
is tongue
placement.)

Jojo E
Throat and Body Front
(Cut 1)

Direction of Fur

Jojo D
Back of Head
(Cut 1)

Direction of Fur

Scale: 1 square = 3/4"

chapter eleven

Puppet Skit: Jasper's Disaster

Part 1: The Voice of Temptation

Cast: Jasper (boy puppet)
Mom
Temptation (mean-looking puppet in a red cape)

Props: Spray foam rug cleaner

Scene: Kitchen

MOM: Alright, Jasper. I'm going to Mrs. Goldberg's for awhile. Are you sure you'll be alright here by yourself?

JASPER: Yes, Mom! I'll be alright! I'm nine whole years old already! Gimme a break, will ya? *[He sighs with disgust]*

MOM: You watch your attitude, young man.

JASPER: Yes Ma'am.

MOM: Now, you can have anything you want for a snack today. And remember the rules of the house:

MOM and JASPER: "Don't use the stove, Don't play with the appliances, and Only watch the TV shows we allow here."

MOM: Can I trust you , Jasper?

JASPER: Yes Ma'am! You can trust me! *[He turns to the audience and giggles nervously.]*

MOM: That's my boy! Now, I'm counting on everything being in order when I get back. You can have anything you want for a snack today. And if you have any problems, call Mrs. Thomas next door, all right?

JASPER: Okey dokey!

MOM: Bye, dear.

Mom exits.

JASPER: Wow! I'm all alone in the house for the first time! This is great! I can eat anything I want! Hmmm. I want…a milk shake! Yeah! That sounds great! *[He opens the refrigerator door]* Oh, I forgot. Milkshakes have to be made in the blender. Mom said I can't use the appliances. But I want a milkshake. How can I eat anything I want if I can't MAKE anything I want? Boy, this is no fun! This is no fun at all. *[TEMPTATION appears at top of puppet stage or directly behind Jasper's shoulder.]* All these silly rules and regulations. It bugs me…

TEMPTATION: Hey there, big guy.

JASPER: Who said that?

TEMPTATION: Give you one guess.

JASPER: Well, I can't see you. I can only hear you inside me. Keep talking and maybe I can recognize the voice.

TEMPTATION: All right. Say, I hear you wanna make a milkshake but your mother won't let you use the blender. I think that's ridiculous!

JASPER: Hey, I like your voice. You must be the voice of intelligent thinking.

TEMPTATION: Exactly! *[to the audience]* He doesn't know that I'm really the voice of temptation. I'm gonna get that kid to disobey. I'm good at that. Remember when I wore a snake outfit in the Garden of Eden? Eve liked listening to me too. Watch me work on this kid.

JASPER: What do you think I should do? I really WANT a milkshake right now. And it's in my power to have one. The only think stopping me is Mom's silly old rule.

TEMPTATION: And it IS a silly rule, Jasper. Look atcha. You're nine years old already. You should be able to turn on a blender. You won't get cut or nothin', unless you do something stupid like put your hand in there—and you wouldn't do that, would you?

JASPER: No way!

TEMPTATION: And you can't get electrocuted just by pushing a button. So go ahead and make that shake. You can wash the blender out, and Mom will never know! Besides, you've always wanted to put something in that blender and watch it bubble and swirl. Go on, big guy! Enjoy! Enjoy!

TEMPTATION disappears.

JASPER: Yeah…yeah, I will! Yeah. I'm nine years old. A guy oughta be able to do a few things by my age. Mom's just a bit old fashioned. I can do it. Okay. Here's the

milk…here's the blender…add a few ice cubes…some sugar…and vanilla…and just push the ole button there and—

The sound of a blender motor interrupts. Meanwhile, another puppeteer sprays Jasper from below with aerosol foam rug cleaner—it won't harm the puppets.

JASPER: Help! Wait! How do I stop this thing? *[It stops.]* Oh, no! I forgot to put on the lid! What a mess! Now I have to spend my whole afternoon alone cleaning Mom's kitchen so she won't find out.

VOICE OF MOM: Jasper, I'm home!

JASPER: *[Shocked]* Aaaagh! No! Wait! I mean—you can't come in! You can't—

MOM: *[entering]* Mrs. Goldberg's poodle was sick and I—*[she sees the mess]* JASPER JEFFERSON MILLER THE THIRD! WHAT ON EARTH HAVE YOU DONE?

JASPER: I was making a…a milkshake. *[He holds out his hand with froth as if to offer her some]* Vanilla?

MOM: *[slowly approaching, backing him into the side wall]* JAAASSPPERRR, I'm going to—

JASPER: I'm sorry, Mom! I won't do it again! Lord God in heaven, have mercy on me!

MOM: Your soul might belong to Jesus, son, but your backside belongs to me!

Besides, God IS having mercy on you by letting me come home early so I could catch you in this deed and steer you right! So don't ask him to remove your punishment, young man! You will be punished, count on it! *[she suddenly snaps into a calm mode, and looks at the audience and speaks in a comedic angelic tone for a moment]* But first, let's discuss what you did so you'll know why you're getting it! Come on, young man! Upstairs! *[to herself as she exits]* I will be calm…I WILL be calm…I will be CALM…

Part 2: Resisting Temptation

Cast: Jasper (boy puppet)
  Mom
  Allison the babysitter (teenage puppet)
  Temptation (mean-looking puppet in a red cape)

Props: Cardboard TV

Scene: The family room

MOM: I'm leaving now. Thank you for babysitting on such short notice, Allison. I just couldn't leave Jasper home alone—he's not quite ready yet.

ALLISON: Like, it's no problem Mrs. Miller. Like, I'm sure I'll enjoy taking care of little Jasper here. I mean, he's so cute and all.

JASPER: Yuck.

ALLISON: Besides, cash speaks louder than

little twink—I mean tweet little pookie bears like cute little Jasper Miller.

MOM: Uh… *[takes a breath]* Okay, well I'm off. Goodbye, darling. Listen to Allison and help her keep the rules of the house. Try not to give her a hard time. So long.

JASPER: *[dryly]* Bye, Mom.

Mom exits.

ALLISON: So. It's like three whole hours here with you. Aren't you a little old for a babysitter? I mean, like, I was staying home alone when I was seven already.

JASPER: At night?

ALLISON: Sure.

JASPER: Did you keep all the rules?

ALLISON: We didn't have rules. I did whatever I wanted. And I still do. Hey, wanna watch TV?

JASPER: Sure.

ALLISON: Cool. Just in time. Streetwise is on. My favorite TV show.

JASPER: But that's one of the programs we can't watch here. Mom said.

ALLISON: Listen, kid. It's YOUR family's rule, not mine. I'm watching it.

JASPER: But this is our house. And it says

right here on the list Mom wrote, "Programs we do not allow in our home: Streetwise, Fallen Angels—

ALLISON: Listen, kid, I do not care. Like, read my lips, okay? I DO NOT CARE. Got it? So like quit interrupting and have a seat.

JASPER: You mean, I can watch it with you?

ALLISON: Like, only if you promise not to tell your Mom. Listen, I'm gonna go get some popcorn while the commercial's on. I'll be right back.

Allison exits.

JASPER: Wow! I always wanted to watch Streetwise! Everybody says it's cool. Well, almost everybody. Some of my church friends say it promotes non-Christian values. That's what Mom says, too. She says it makes people look cool doing things that are wrong. Hmm.

TEMPTATION appears, as in Part 1.

TEMPTATION: Hey there, big guy.

JASPER: Who said that? Who's talking to me?

TEMPTATION: Let's just say, it's…how'd you put it…the voice of "intelligent thinkin.".

JASPER: Go on.

TEMPTATION: Jasper. So you wanna watch Streetwise. And your church friends say it promotes "non-Christian values". I think that's square. Yeah. I think you oughta watch that show. Don't you?

JASPER: But it's a forbidden show in my home. I'd be disobedient if I watched it.

TEMPTATION: Jasper, Jasper, Jasper. Nobody's gonna know! It's your own secret! Go ahead. Enjoy! Enjoy!

JASPER: *[recognizing the voice at last]* Hey! I know your voice! You're not the voice of intelligent thinking! You're just the wiley ole voice of temptation, trying to get me to do the wrong thing. Well you got me in trouble one time today, and I'm not listening to you anymore! I'm gonna obey my mother! So there!

TEMPTATION: *[to audience]* Brother! Business is terrible these days! Wonder if they're hirin' at McDonald's???

TEMPTATION exits.

JASPER: Wow! Imagine that! Tempted two times in one day! Boy, life's gettin' rough! But I sure feel good inside knowing I made the right choice. I'm not gonna watch that show, because Mom says it promotes non-Christian values. And that means they make things look right that are wrong. I don't wanna be duped.

VOICE OF ALLISON: Hey, kid, is the commercial over yet?

JASPER: I don't know. 'Cause I'm not looking at it. And I'm not listening to it, either.

Allison enters.

ALLISON: You little brat! I asked you a question! Did you just sass me, or what?

JASPER: I'm just stating a fact. I'm not watching that show because it's forbidden in my home. I'm going to my room.

ALLISON: Be a nerd, I don't care!

Time passes, then Mom returns.

MOM: So here's your money, Allison. And thanks again for babysitting on such short notice.

ALLISON: *[looking at the money]* Hey, a tip, too! That's cool. Thanks!

MOM: You deserve it!

ALLISON: Anytime. Later.

MOM: Goodbye, Allison.

The door closes. Jasper enters from the other side.

JASPER: Mom.

MOM: Jasper! What are you doing out of bed? It's 11:30.

JASPER: I've been in my room almost since you left. I— I couldn't sleep.

MOM: Did Allison have to send you to your room? What did you do this time?

JASPER: It's not what I did. It's what Allison did. She watched a TV show that we don't allow here.

MOM: What? You mean, one on the list I gave her?

JASPER: Streetwise.

MOM: (gasps) Streetwise? But that's inappropriate for— And I even tipped that girl! She let you watch that—

JASPER: I didn't watch it, Mom. I could have, but I didn't. I knew it would be wrong, so I went to my room. And stayed there.

MOM: Oh, Jasper! I'm so proud of you!

JASPER: I'm kind proud of myself! I learned to obey, even when it's hard! I want to please Jesus. And I want to please you too, Mom.

Mom faints backward.

JASPER: Mom? Mom? Should I call 911?

Mom gets up.
MOM: Are you kidding? I've never felt better! Come on, Jasper. I'll tuck you in!

chapter twelve

Puppet Skit: It's Not Neat To Cheat

Part 1: The Test

Cast: *Jasper (boy puppet)*
Mr. Severe (teacher)
Temptation
various studentss

Scene: A classroom. Use as many puppets as you can for students. Have the students face the teacher, who, in turn, faces the audience.

MR SEVERE: Now class, the test is about to begin. I hope you all studied the way you were supposed to. If so, you should all do very well. Now please write your answers neatly in the blanks. Ready? Begin.

Heads bow as if they're writing.

JASPER: *[turns to audience]* Boy, why didn't I study last night? Instead, I watched TV. It was an old Charlie Brown cartoon. I couldn't pass it up! They won't show it again for years! *[pauses]* Betcha Kirby studied. *[pauses]* He'll probabaly get an A. He always gets an A. He'll get an A,

and I'll flunk, and I'll be grounded forever. What am I gonna do?

Tempter enters.

TEMPTER: Hey there, big guy!

JASPER: Huh? I heard a voice in my mind. Wonder who it could be.

TEMPTER: I'm the voice of, uh…wisdom and understanding. Yeah, that's it. Wisdom and understanding.

JASPER: Boy, I could sure use some wisdom and understanding right now. I don't know the answers to this test. I didn't study.

TEMPTER: I know. But you had a good excuse. I mean, Charlie Brown is a classic. You HAD to watch that show instead of study.

JASPER: Yeah, but now I have to pay.

TEMPTER: Negatory, my man! Now you have to PLAY!

JASPER: Play?

TEMPTER: Play the game of chance. You have one chance to ace this test, and one chance only. What are you gonna do about it, hmmm?

JASPER: Y-y-you mean, cheat?

TEMPTER: Ooh, strong language there—and not necessary. You wouldn't be cheating if you copied Kirby's answers, my man. You're just covering yourself, just this once. It's not like you're making a habit of this kind of thing. Besides, Kirby is really no smarter than you, so you're not taking anything from him that you can't get by studying a little extra tonight, just to make it square, you know?

JASPER: Yeah...I could study extra tonight to make up for it! I can study what I should of studied last night, then every thing will be squared up!

TEMPTER: Exactly! Now glance over there to your right and copy those answers. It's an easy A!

JASPER: Yeah. *[pauses]* Yeah! It's the only thing to do. Mr. Severe expects me to do well. I always do. So he won't suspect a thing when Kirby and I get our usual A's. Yeah!

Jasper copies. Throw in a small musical interlude here while the kids do their test. Keep it short—only about 10 seconds.

MR. SEVERE: All right class, time is up. Please pass your papers to the front of the class and you are dismissed.

KIRBY: *[to Jasper]* So, Jasper, how do you think you did on the test?

JASPER: Easiest test I ever took.

KIRBY: Wish I could say the same.

JASPER: *[startled]* What do you mean?

KIRBY: I'm in big trouble, Jasper. I didn't study last night. I watched Charlie Brown instead. I just made up all my answers.

Jasper jerks at the news, then swoons and moans.

KIRBY: What's wrong?

JASPER: Ooh, I don't feel so good. I think I need to go home. See ya.

KIRBY: Bye. Sorry you're not feeling well. I'll pray for you.

JASPER: Pray? Yeah. Yeah. Pray for me. I think I'm gonna be sick. Bye.

KIRBY: Bye.

They exit.

Part 2: Jasper's Choice

Cast: *Jasper (boy puppet)*
Temptation
Voice of Truth

Scene: Jasper is alone with himself. Scene can be just a blank curtain.

JASPER: Boy, what am I gonna do now? I cheated on my test. ME! I CHEATED! I can't believe I fell into temptation like that! What am I gonna do now?

A gentle voice is heard, preferably with a bit of reverb through a speaker.

VOICE OF TRUTH: Tell the truth.

JASPER: Who said that? Who's talking to me?

VOICE OF TRUTH: The voice of Truth, Jasper.

JASPER: How do I know you're not the voice of temptation? I don't know what voices to listen to anymore.

VOICE OF TRUTH: The thoughts that come from the Lord never tempt you to do things that are wrong, Jasper. You can always compare them to what the Bible says. You feel you should tell the truth. Does that sound like the wrong thing to do?

JASPER: No, but it will bring me great bodily harm! I could get grounded!

VOICE OF TRUTH: Which is worse? Getting grounded today, or finding yourself far from God tomorrow?

JASPER: I don't want to get far away from God. I love God. And he loves me. I can't let him down. I've got to tell the truth. I'll take my punishment, but at least Mom and Dad and Mr. Severe will be able to trust me again. And God will be pleased.

Another voice is heard, which causes Jasper to look the other way.

TEMPTATION: Wait just a minute! Jasper! What do you think you're doing? You can't listen to this goody-two-shoes! You'll get creamed by your old man and all your friends will find out you cheated and they're gonna call you names and avoid you like the plague! I suggest you get out of this mess by saying that Kirby copied YOUR paper. Nobody can prove it isn't so!

Jasper turns in the other direction, as if the Voice of Truth is on one side, and Temptation is on the other.

VOICE OF TRUTH: Don't believe it, Jasper!

JASPER: Now I'm confused! I want to tell the truth, but it seems so easy to just lie and get out of it!

VOICE OF TRUTH: This is a battle for your soul, Jasper. Don't let evil win!

JASPER: But I'm not strong enough to fight alone! Lord Jesus, help me!

TEMPTATION: Aaaagh! That name! I can't take it! I have to get outta here! Yeeeoww!

VOICE OF TRUTH: You did the right thing, Jasper. You called on the name of the Lord Jesus. And he is helping you, even now!

JASPER: Yeah! I think I can tell the truth after all! I'm gonna go tell Dad right now!

NOTES